The Way of a Pilgrim

THE
WAY OF A PILGRIM

Translated from the Russian by
R. M. FRENCH

Introduction by
Metropolitan Anthony of Sourozh

LONDON
S · P · C · K

First Published 1930
Published by S.P.C.K. 1941
New edition 1954
Reprinted 1960, 1965
Paperback edition with new Introduction 1972
Reprinted 1973

Printed in Great Britain by
The Camelot Press Ltd, London and Southampton

SBN 281 02722 6

Introduction by
Metropolitan Anthony of
Sourozh

"The Way of a Pilgrim" has become in the West a classic of Russian Orthodox spirituality. No book to my knowledge has inspired more people to set out to discover the inner springs that nurture the life of Orthodox Christians and to learn the practice of the Jesus Prayer. It has been for many, as it was for me when I read it in my late teens, a revelation about the life of prayer.

I should, however, like to attract the attention of the reader to two things: firstly, that the book was written by a Pilgrim endowed with a simplicity and wholeness which are rare at any epoch but very difficult to experience in our own day. Therefore I would like to warn against any attempt simply to ape the Pilgrim, free from family life, unhampered by any concern, even for his own survival. Always on the move and completely unattached, the Pilgrim had an inner freedom which few enjoy or would probably care to possess at the cost he paid for it.

Secondly, the Pilgrim learnt the Jesus Prayer from a master and it was his guidance and his teaching that enabled him to read *The Philokalia* with, as St. Paul says, the "eyes of the spirit". Like every book of spirituality *The Philokalia* (an anthology of Orthodox spiritual writings both ascetic and mystical) needs a key for its understanding: it is given first and foremost by belonging in doctrine and in worship to the Church which gave it birth; but even within the Church grave and damaging mistakes will only be avoided by those who will wholeheartedly and daringly wish to learn from one who has had personal experience of what is taught and disclosed there.

Man is called to be by nature one with the created world and to become by grace one with God, uniting the creator with the creature. This involves not only realizing the integrity of man redeemed and renewed in our Lord, not only the standing face to face of the new man with God, but in the synergic work of God and man, the transfiguration of the human being making man, as St. Peter expresses it, a "partaker of divine nature", not by a metaphorical but by a real divinization.

Man's aim, the end and vocation set before him, is that through and beyond his own union with God, he should make this transcendent yet ever-present God (who enfolds and penetrates all, in whom we live and move and have our being, but who remains unknown to the world, unknowable indeed from without) interior and immanent in man and through man in the world; united with his creature indissolubly, though without confusion, distinct yet not alien, still himself, still personal, still God—yet closer to the soul than breathing itself.

This aim, this vocation of union with God, is central to the Prayer in the Name of Jesus. Brief in form, it leads the soul to concentration and sets it face to face with God. Its tenor is such as will fix and bind into one all the forces of man, spiritual, mental, and corporal, in that single act of perfect devotion—loving adoration. It endows the being with absolute stability. At the same time it strips the soul of all subjectivity, all self-seeking, and sets it in the objectivity of the divine. It is both the path and the culmination of renunciation and self-denial.

Prayer originates in an act of faith which confronts us with the Uncreated, the personal and living God. It depends on no artifice and can be won neither by ruse nor by force: it is a free gift of self on both sides. And all true prayer—that is, prayer offered in perfect humility, in the absence of all self-preoccupation, by a suppliant who has made his peace with God, his conscience, and the whole cosmos and has forever abandoned himself to God —is sooner or later animated by the grace of the Holy Spirit. It then becomes the ferment of every action and serves as its criterion, becomes the *whole* of life, ceases to be an activity to become *being* itself. Only then does it fix its abode in the heart, enabling the suppliant to adore God from the depths of his heart and unite with him. Moreover, and this is fundamental, the techniques which facilitate detection and location of this point artificially are none of them designed to produce prayer, still less to engender somatopsychic emotional complexes as the fallacious object of mystical experience. Their purpose is to teach the *novice*, for whom they are intended, *where* this optimum centre of attention is, so that when the moment arrives he may recognize this as his prayer's point of origin and remain there. Then, too, the establishment of attention at this point creates the conditions most favourable to depth and stability of prayer. While it is true that genuine prayer does utilize this physical point of attention, it is also important to remember that attention may be fixed there quite apart from prayer: like any artifice, this can take one only as far as it goes and guarantees one nothing further.

The body then is not a productive agency but an objective criterion; what is demanded of it, as of the mind, is silence and return to unity. It is active, but not creative; like everything in man, it is fertile soil that awaits the sowing. As an integral part of the total man, the body too shall bear its fruits of holiness, being called to transfiguration, resurrection, and eternal life.

For the master, the body with its every movement is a precious prospector's instrument, enabling him to discern certain states at a glance even while their psychological context is still uncertain or the disciple still unskilled in perceiving the finer points of his inner life. The science of the Fathers in this matter is therefore not instruction about prayer or even about the inner life but an ascesis and a test of attention. Hence the importance of a master guiding the beginner both in his inner life and in his bodily exercises, checking one by the other, and keeping the novice from mistaking for the effects of grace the natural results of his ascesis.

Any technical or interpretative error may actually have the most woeful consequences, as has been shown by the experience of the fourteenth-century monks of Athos and of all the proud and unwary who have believed themselves able to use the somatic techniques without guidance.

Use of the bodily exercise thus unquestionably requires

Introduction

a master who is both experienced and vigilant. On the disciple's part are required great simplicity and an active and confident abandon. The novice's difficulties mount, as do his dangers, with his own psychic complexity and with the disposition fostered by our modern education to "watch oneself live" instead of living.

This ascetical discipline fashions a mould and it is meaningless apart from the content enclosed therein. It is inseparably associated with a mental ascesis. But all technical exercises constitute not contemplative prayer, only a purely negative liberating asceticism which prepares a *form* for it. Once attention is unified and localized at the point of perfect concentration, the spiritual work only begins. In it prayer itself is a stabilizing factor; it should not destroy unity by calling into play only one part of the human being—intellect or feeling or will—but rather in itself make for concentration and unity and be the means of realizing union with God in mind, body, and soul.

In short, the doctrinal and spiritual wealth of the Jesus Prayer is infinite: it is both a summary and the whole of the faith whose enigma is solved in Christ. Not only does it speak to us of God, but with its ceaseless invocation, its profound cry of the creature toward his God, it brings forth the presence of Christ it has invoked. He himself comes to his creature, at whose request he works the one miracle longed for; he abides, unites himself with the creature, so that it is no longer the creature who lives, but Christ who lives in him.

There are a certain number of preliminary conditions

that must be satisfied by the man who wishes to engage in the Jesus Prayer, with God's help and under the direction of his spiritual father. First, an awareness, clear or confused, of the horror into which is plunged the man who is "outside God", walled up in the deadly isolation of his ego. As Theophan the Recluse teaches: "a self-centred man is like a thin shaving of wood curling up around the void of his inner nothingness, cut off alike from the cosmos and the Creator of all things". Secondly there must be the belief that life is found in God alone, and thirdly there must be the will for conversion, that is to say, for the spiritual volte-face which makes us essentially and irrevocably strangers to a world sundered from God and sets us on a new plane of existence, that of God himself and the world in God.

Thus, as he embarks on his course, the Christian must make his peace with God, with his own conscience, with men and things; relinquish all care about himself, firmly purpose to forget himself, not to know himself, to kill in himself all greed, even for spiritual things, in order to know nothing but God alone.

"Leave as one leaveth a dream, the love of this world and of sweetness; cast away thy cares, strip thyself of vain thoughts, renounce thy body; for prayer is naught else save only to be a stranger in the visible world and in the invisible. What is there in the heavens that draweth me? Nothing. And what should I desire of Thee on earth? Nothing, save that I should ever cling to Thee in undistracted prayer. Some make riches the object of their desires, others glory. For me, I desire nothing save to cling to God and put in Him alone the hope of my soul stripped of passion." (St. John of the Ladder.)

Henceforward the worshipper must free himself from the bondage of the world by unconditional obedience— joyful, total, humble, and immediate; he must in all simplicity seek God, without hiding any of his wretchedness, without founding any hope on himself, in this active self-abandonment to God which is the spirit of watchfulness in humility, in veneration, with a sincere will to be converted, ready to die rather than give up the search.

There is no doubt that the most characteristic feature of the Jesus Prayer and of the hesychast (quietist) tradition in which it is grounded, the most precious legacy it has left to the Orthodox, is this indissoluble union of a physical and mental ascetic technique of minute exactness and extreme strictness in the demands it makes, with a high affirmation of the fundamental worthlessness of all technique and all artificial means in the mystery of the union of the soul with God—the mystery of mutual self-giving in love, in the fullness of liberty. Hence it is possible to use all ascetic methods, but with discernment, freedom, boldness; "all is lawful for me, but all is not expedient". This filial liberty and strict fidelity is the attitude of the Orthodox Church.

Preface

THE Russian title of this book may be literally translated "Candid Narratives of a Pilgrim to His Spiritual Father." The title chosen for the English version explains itself and is meant to cover the twofold interest of the book. It is the story of some of the Pilgrim's experiences as he made his *way* from place to place in Russia and Siberia. No one can miss the charm of these travel notes in the simple directness with which they are told and the clear-cut sketches of people which they contain.

It is also the story of the Pilgrim's learning and practising, and on occasion teaching to others, a *way* of praying. Upon this, the *hesychast* method of prayer, much might be said, and not everyone will be in sympathy with it. But everyone will appreciate the sincerity of his conviction and few probably will doubt the reality of his experience. Strongly contrasted as the method may be with an ordinary religious Englishman's habits of devotion, for another type of soul it may still be the expression of vivid realisation of the truth "for me to live is Christ."

Those who wish to read more of the *hesychast* method of prayer and its connection with the great Byzantine Mystic, St. Simeon the New Theologian, who lived from 949 to 1022, may be referred to *Orientalia Christiana*, Vol. IX, No. 36 (June and July, 1927).

The events described in the book appear to belong to a Russia prior to the Liberation of the Serfs, which took place in 1861. The reference to the Crimean War in the *Fourth Narrative* gives 1853 as the other limit of time. Between those two dates the Pilgrim arrived at Irkutsk, where he found a Spiritual Father. He tells the latter how he came to learn the Prayer of Jesus, partly from the oral teaching of his *starets*, and after the loss of his *starets*, from his own study of *The Philokalia*. This is the substance of the first two *Narratives*, which are divided by the death of the *starets*.

The *Third Narrative* is very short, and tells, in response to his Spiritual Father's enquiries, the Pilgrim's earlier personal history and what led him to become a Pilgrim at all.

It was his intention to go on from Irkutsk to Jerusalem, and indeed he had actually started. But a chance encounter led to a postponement of his departure for some days, and during that time he relates the further experiences of his pilgrim life which make up the *Fourth Narrative*.

Of the Pilgrim's identity nothing is known. In some way his manuscript, or a copy of it, came into the hands of a monk on Mount Athos, in whose possession it was found by the Abbot of St. Michael's Monastery at Kazan. The Abbot copied the manuscript, and from his copy the book was printed at Kazan in 1884.

In recent years copies of this (until April, 1930, the only) edition have become exceedingly difficult to get. There appear to be only three or four copies in existence outside Russia, and I am deeply indebted to friends in Denmark and Bulgaria for the loan of copies from which this translation was made. I am very grateful also to the Reverend N. Behr, Proto-priest of the Russian Church in London, for so kindly reading through the manuscript of my translation.

A very few notes have been added and placed at the end of the book. They are chiefly to explain one or two words which it seemed best not to attempt to turn into English.

R. M. F.

1

BY the grace of God I am a Christian man, by my
actions a great sinner, and by calling a homeless
wanderer of the humblest birth who roams from place to
place. My worldly goods are a knapsack with some dried
bread in it on my back, and in my breast-pocket a Bible.
And that is all.

On the 24th Sunday after Pentecost I went to church
to say my prayers there during the Liturgy. The first
Epistle of St. Paul to the Thessalonians was being read,
and among other words I heard these—"*Pray without
ceasing.*" It was this text, more than any other, which
forced itself upon my mind, and I began to think how
it was possible to pray without ceasing, since a man has
to concern himself with other things also in order to
make a living. I looked at my Bible, and with my own
eyes read the words which I had heard, *i.e.*, that we ought
always, at all times and in all places, to pray with up-
lifted hands. I thought and thought, but knew not
what to make of it. "What ought I to do?" I thought.
"Where shall I find someone to explain it to me? I
will go to the churches where famous preachers are to be
heard; perhaps there I shall hear something which will
throw light on it for me." I did so. I heard a number
of very fine sermons on prayer; what prayer is, how
much we need it, and what its fruits are; but no one
said how one could succeed in prayer. I heard a sermon

on spiritual prayer, and unceasing prayer, but how it was to be done was not pointed out.

Thus listening to sermons failed to give me what I wanted, and having had my fill of them without gaining understanding, I gave up going to hear public sermons. I settled on another plan—by God's help to look for some experienced and skilled person who would give me in conversation that teaching about unceasing prayer which drew me so urgently.

For a long time I wandered through many places. I read my Bible always, and everywhere I asked whether there was not in the neighbourhood a spiritual teacher, a devout and experienced guide, to be found. One day I was told that in a certain village a gentleman had long been living and seeking the salvation of his soul. He had a chapel in his house. He never left his estate, and he spent his time in prayer and reading devotional books. Hearing this, I ran rather than walked to the village named. I got there and found him.

" What do you want of me ? " he asked.

"I have heard that you are a devout and clever person", said I. " In God's name please explain to me the meaning of the Apostle's words, ' *Pray without ceasing.*' How is it possible to pray without ceasing ? I want to know so much, but I cannot understand it at all."

He was silent for a while and looked at me closely. Then he said : " Ceaseless interior prayer is a continual yearning of the human spirit towards God. To succeed in this consoling exercise we must pray more often to God to teach us to pray without ceasing. Pray more, and pray more fervently. It is prayer itself which will reveal to you how it can be achieved unceasingly; but it will take some time."

So saying, he had food brought to me, gave me money for my journey, and let me go.

He did not explain the matter.

Again I set off. I thought and thought, I read and read, I dwelt over and over again upon what this man had said to me, but I could not get to the bottom of it. Yet so greatly did I wish to understand that I could not sleep at night.

I walked at least a hundred and twenty-five miles, and then I came to a large town, a provincial capital, where I saw a monastery. At the inn where I stopped I heard it said that the Abbot was a man of great kindness, devout and hospitable. I went to see him. He met me in a very friendly manner, asked me to sit down, and offered me refreshment.

" I do not need refreshment, holy Father," I said, " but I beg you to give me some spiritual teaching. How can I save my soul ? "

" What ? Save your soul ? Well, live according to the commandments, say your prayers, and you will be saved."

" But I hear it said that we should pray without ceasing, and I don't know how to pray without ceasing. I cannot even understand what unceasing prayer means. I beg you, Father, explain this to me."

" I don't know how to explain further, dear brother. But, stop a moment, I have a little book, and it is

3

explained there." And he handed me St. Dmitri's book on *The Spiritual Education of the Inner Man*, saying, " Look, read this page."

I began to read as follows : " The words of the Apostle ' *Pray without ceasing* ' should be understood as referring to the creative prayer of the understanding. The understanding can always be reaching out towards God, and pray to Him unceasingly."

" But ", I asked, " what is the method by which the understanding can always be turned towards God, never be disturbed, and pray without ceasing ? "

" It is very difficult, even for one to whom God Himself gives such a gift ", replied the Abbot.

He did not give me the explanation.

I spent the night at his house, and in the morning, thanking him for his kindly hospitality, I went on my way ; where to, I did not know myself. My failure to understand made me sad, and by way of comforting myself I read my Bible. In this way I followed the main road for five days.

At last towards evening I was overtaken by an old man who looked like a cleric of some sort. In answer to my question he told me that he was a monk belonging to a monastery some six miles off the main road. He asked me to go there with him. " We take in pilgrims," said he, " and give them rest and food with devout persons in the guest house." I did not feel like going. So in reply I said that my peace of mind in no way depended upon my finding a resting-place, but upon finding spiritual teaching. Neither was I running

4

after food, for I had plenty of dried bread in my knapsack.

" What sort of spiritual teaching are you wanting to get ? " he asked me. " What is it puzzling you ? Come now ! Do come to our house, dear brother. We have *startsi* [1]* of ripe experience well able to give guidance to your soul and to set it upon the true path, in the light of the word of God and the writings of the holy Fathers."

" Well, it's like this, Father", said I. " About a year ago, while I was at the Liturgy, I heard a passage from the Epistles which bade men pray without ceasing. Failing to understand, I began to read my Bible, and there also in many places I found the divine command that we ought to pray at all times, in all places ; not only while about our business, not only while awake, but even during sleep, ' *I sleep, but my heart waketh.*' This surprised me very much, and I was at a loss to understand how it could be carried out and in what way it was to be done. A burning desire and thirst for knowledge awoke in me. Day and night the matter was never out of my mind. So I began to go to churches and to listen to sermons. But however many I heard, from not one of them did I get any teaching about how to pray without ceasing. They always talked about getting ready for prayer, or about its fruits and the like, without teaching one *how* to pray without ceasing, or what such prayer means. I have often read the Bible and there made sure of what I have heard. But meanwhile I have not reached

* The number refers to the notes at the end of the book.

the understanding that I long for, and so to this hour I am still uneasy and in doubt."

Then the old man crossed himself and spoke. " Thank God, my dear brother, for having revealed to you this unappeasable desire for unceasing interior prayer. Recognise in it the call of God, and calm yourself. Rest assured that what has hitherto been accomplished in you is the testing of the harmony of your own will with the voice of God. It has been granted to you to understand that the heavenly light of unceasing interior prayer is attained neither by the wisdom of this world, nor by the mere outward desire for knowledge, but that on the contrary it is found in poverty of spirit and in active experience in simplicity of heart. That is why it is not surprising that you have been unable to hear anything about the essential work of prayer, and to acquire the knowledge by which ceaseless activity in it is attained. Doubtless a great deal has been preached about prayer, and there is much about it in the teaching of various writers. But since for the most part all their reasonings are based upon speculation and the working of natural wisdom, and not upon active experience, they sermonise about the qualities of prayer, rather than about the nature of the thing itself. One argues beautifully about the necessity of prayer, another about its power and the blessings which attend it, a third again about the things which lead to perfection in prayer, *i.e.*, about the absolute necessity of zeal, an attentive mind, warmth of heart, purity of thought, reconciliation with one's enemies, humility, contrition, and so on. But what is prayer?

6

The Way of a Pilgrim

And how does one learn to pray? Upon these questions, primary and essential as they are, one very rarely gets any precise enlightenment from present-day preachers. For these questions are more difficult to understand than all their arguments that I have just spoken of, and require mystical knowledge, not simply the learning of the schools. And the most deplorable thing of all is that the vain wisdom of the world compels them to apply the human standard to the divine. Many people reason quite the wrong way round about prayer, thinking that good actions and all sorts of preliminary measures render us capable of prayer. But quite the reverse is the case, it is prayer which bears fruit in good works and all the virtues. Those who reason so, take, incorrectly, the fruits and the results of prayer for the means of attaining it, and this is to depreciate the power of prayer. And it is quite contrary to Holy Scripture, for the Apostle Paul says, '*I exhort therefore that first of all supplications be made*' (1 Tim., ii, 1). The first thing laid down in the Apostle's words about prayer is that the work of prayer comes before everything else: '*I exhort therefore that first of all* . . .' The Christian is bound to perform many good works, but before all else what he ought to do is to pray, for without prayer no other good work whatever can be accomplished. Without prayer he cannot find the way to the Lord, he cannot understand the truth, he cannot crucify the flesh with its passions and lusts, his heart cannot be enlightened with the light of Christ, he cannot be savingly united to God. None of those things can be effected unless they are preceded by constant prayer. I say 'constant,' for the perfection of prayer does not lie within our power; as the Apostle Paul says, ' *For we know not what we should pray for as we ought* ' (Rom. viii, 26). Consequently it is just to pray often, to pray always, which falls within our power as the means of attaining purity of prayer, which is the mother of all spiritual blessings. ' Capture the Mother, and she will bring you the children,' said St. Isaac the Syrian. Learn first to acquire the power of prayer and you will easily practise all the other virtues. But those who know little of this from practical experience and the profoundest teaching of the holy Fathers, have no clear knowledge of it and speak of it but little."

During this talk, we had almost reached the monastery. And so as not to lose touch with this wise old man, and to get what I wanted more quickly, I hastened to say, " Be so kind, Reverend Father, as to show me what prayer without ceasing means and how it is learnt. I see you know all about these things."

He took my request kindly and asked me into his cell. " Come in," said he ; " I will give you a volume of the holy Fathers from which with God's help you can learn about prayer clearly and in detail."

We went into his cell and he began to speak as follows. " The continuous interior Prayer of Jesus is a constant uninterrupted calling upon the divine Name of Jesus with the lips, in the spirit, in the heart ; while forming a mental picture of His constant presence, and imploring His grace, during every occupation, at all times, in all places, even during sleep. The appeal is couched in

8

these terms, ' Lord Jesus Christ, have mercy on me.' One who accustoms himself to this appeal experiences as a result so deep a consolation and so great a need to offer the prayer always, that he can no longer live without it, and it will continue to voice itself within him of its own accord. Now do you understand what prayer without ceasing is ? ''

" Yes indeed, Father, and in God's name teach me how to gain the habit of it," I cried, filled with joy.

" Read this book," he said. " It is called *The Philokalia*,[2] and it contains the full and detailed science of constant interior prayer, set forth by twenty-five holy Fathers. The book is marked by a lofty wisdom and is so profitable to use that it is considered the foremost and best manual of the contemplative spiritual life. As the revered Nicephorus said, ' It leads one to salvation without labour and sweat.' ''

" Is it then more sublime and holy than the Bible ? '' I asked.

" No, it is not that. But it contains clear explanations of what the Bible holds in secret and which cannot be easily grasped by our short-sighted understanding. I will give you an illustration. The sun is the greatest, the most resplendent and the most wonderful of heavenly luminaries, but you cannot contemplate and examine it simply with unprotected eyes. You have to use a piece of artificial glass which is many millions of times smaller and darker than the sun. But through this little piece of glass you can examine the magnificent monarch of stars, delight in it, and endure its fiery rays. Holy Scripture

9

also is a dazzling sun, and this book, *The Philokalia*, is the piece of glass which we use to enable us to contemplate the sun in its imperial splendour. Listen now, I am going to read you the sort of instruction it gives on unceasing interior prayer."

He opened the book, found the instruction by St. Simeon the New Theologian, and read : " Sit down alone and in silence. Lower your head, shut your eyes, breathe out gently and imagine yourself looking into your own heart. Carry your mind, *i.e.*, your thoughts, from your head to your heart. As you breathe out, say ' Lord Jesus Christ, have mercy on me.' Say it moving your lips gently, or simply say it in your mind. Try to put all other thoughts aside. Be calm, be patient, and repeat the process very frequently."

The old man explained all this to me and illustrated its meaning. We went on reading from *The Philokalia* passages of St. Gregory of Sinai, St. Callistus and St. Ignatius, and what we read from the book the *starets* explained in his own words. I listened closely and with great delight, fixed it in my memory, and tried as far as possible to remember every detail. In this way we spent the whole night together and went to Mattins without having slept at all.

The *starets* sent me away with his blessing and told me that while learning the Prayer I must always come back to him and tell him everything, making a very frank confession and report ; for the inward process could not go on properly and successfully without the guidance of a teacher.

In church I felt a glowing eagerness to take all the pains I could to learn unceasing interior prayer, and I prayed to God to come to my help. Then I began to wonder how I should manage to see my *starets* again for counsel or confession, since leave was not given to remain for more than three days in the monastery guest-house, and there were no houses near.

However, I learned that there was a village between two and three miles from the monastery. I went there to look for a place to live, and to my great happiness God showed me the thing I needed. A peasant hired me for the whole summer to look after his kitchen garden, and what is more gave me the use of a little thatched hut in it where I could live alone. God be praised! I had found a quiet place. And in this manner I took up my abode and began to learn interior prayer in the way I had been shown, and to go to see my *starets* from time to time.

For a week, alone in my garden, I steadily set myself to learn to pray without ceasing exactly as the *starets* had explained. At first things seemed to go very well. But then it tired me very much. I felt lazy and bored and overwhelmingly sleepy, and a cloud of all sorts of other thoughts closed round me. I went in distress to my *starets* and told him the state I was in.

He greeted me in a friendly way and said, " My dear brother, it is the attack of the world of darkness upon you. To that world, nothing is worse than heartfelt prayer on our part. And it is trying by every means to hinder you and to turn you aside from learning the Prayer. But all the same the enemy only does what

God sees fit to allow, and no more than is necessary for us. It would appear that you need a further testing of your humility, and that it is too soon, therefore, for your unmeasured zeal to approach the loftiest entrance to the heart. You might fall into spiritual covetousness. I will read you a little instruction from *The Philokalia* upon such cases."

He turned to the teaching of Nicephorus and read, " ' If after a few attempts you do not succeed in reaching the realm of your heart in the way you have been taught, do what I am about to say, and by God's help you will find what you seek. The faculty of pronouncing words lies in the throat. Reject all other thoughts (you can do this if you will) and allow that faculty to repeat only the following words constantly, " Lord Jesus Christ, have mercy on me." Compel yourself to do it always. If you succeed for a time, then without a doubt your heart also will open to prayer. We know it from experience.'

" There you have the teaching of the holy Fathers on such cases," said my *starets*, " and therefore you ought from to-day onwards to carry out my directions with confidence, and repeat the Prayer of Jesus as often as possible. Here is a rosary. Take it, and to start with say the Prayer three thousand times a day. Whether you are standing or sitting, walking or lying down, continually repeat ' Lord Jesus Christ, have mercy on me.' Say it quietly and without hurry, but without fail exactly three thousand times a day without deliberately increasing or diminishing the number. God will help you and by this means you will reach also the unceasing activity of the heart."

I gladly accepted this guidance and went home and began to carry out faithfully and exactly what my *starets* had bidden. For two days I found it rather difficult, but after that it became so easy and likeable, that as soon as I stopped, I felt a sort of need to go on saying the Prayer of Jesus, and I did it freely and willingly, not forcing myself to it as before.

I reported to my *starets*, and he bade me say the Prayer six thousand times a day, saying, " Be calm, just try as faithfully as possible to carry out the set number of prayers. God will vouchsafe you His grace."

In my lonely hut I said the Prayer of Jesus six thousand times a day for a whole week. I felt no anxiety. Taking no notice of any other thoughts however much they assailed me, I had but one object, *i.e.*, to carry out my *starets'* bidding exactly. And what happened ? I grew so used to my Prayer that when I stopped for a single moment, I felt, so to speak, as though something were missing, as though I had lost something. The very moment I started the Prayer again, it went on easily and joyously. If I met anyone I had no wish to talk to him. All I wanted was to be alone and to say my Prayer, so used to it had I become in a week.

My *starets* had not seen me for ten days. On the eleventh day he came to see me himself, and I told him how things were going. He listened and said, " Now you have got used to the Prayer. See that you preserve the habit and strengthen it. Waste no time, therefore, but make up your mind by God's help from to-day to say the Prayer of Jesus twelve thousand times a day. Remain in your solitude, get up early, go to bed late, and come and ask advice of me every fortnight."

I did as he bade me. The first day I scarcely succeeded in finishing my task of saying twelve thousand prayers by late evening. The second day I did it easily and contentedly. To begin with, this ceaseless saying of the Prayer brought a certain amount of weariness, my tongue felt numbed, I had a stiff sort of feeling in my jaws, I had a feeling at first pleasant but afterwards slightly painful in the roof of my mouth. The thumb of my left hand, with which I counted my beads, hurt a little. I felt a slight inflammation in the whole of that wrist, and even up to the elbow, which was not unpleasant. Moreover, all this aroused me, as it were, and urged me on to frequent saying of the Prayer. For five days I did my set number of twelve thousand prayers, and as I formed the habit I found at the same time pleasure and satisfaction in it.

Early one morning the Prayer woke me up as it were. I started to say my usual morning prayers, but my tongue refused to say them easily or exactly. My whole desire was fixed upon one thing only—to say the Prayer of Jesus, and as soon as I went on with it I was filled with joy and relief. It was as though my lips and my tongue pronounced the words entirely of themselves without any urging from me. I spent the whole day in a state of the greatest contentment, I felt as though I was cut off from everything else. I lived as though in another world, and I easily finished my twelve thousand prayers by the early evening. I felt very much like still going on with them, but I did not dare to go beyond the number my *starets* had set me. Every day following I went on in the same way with my calling on the Name of Jesus Christ, and that with great readiness and liking. Then I went to see my *starets* and told him everything frankly and in detail.

He heard me out and then said, " Be thankful to God that this desire for the Prayer and this facility in it have been manifested in you. It is a natural consequence which follows constant effort and spiritual achievement. So a machine to the principal wheel of which one gives a drive, works for a long while afterwards by itself; but if it is to go on working still longer, one must oil it and give it another drive. Now you see with what admirable gifts God in His love for mankind has endowed even the bodily nature of man. You see what feelings can be produced even outside a state of grace in a soul which is sinful and with passions unsubdued, as you yourself have experienced. But how wonderful, how delightful and how consoling a thing it is when God is pleased to grant the gift of self-acting spiritual prayer, and to cleanse the soul from all sensuality ! It is a condition which is impossible to describe, and the discovery of this mystery of prayer is a foretaste on earth of the bliss of Heaven. Such happiness is reserved for those who seek after God in the simplicity of a loving heart. Now I give you my permission to say your Prayer as often as you wish and as often as you can. Try to devote every moment you are awake to the Prayer, call on the Name of Jesus Christ without counting the number of times, and submit yourself humbly to the will of God, looking to Him for help. I am sure He will not forsake you, and that He will lead you into the right path."

Under this guidance I spent the whole summer in ceaseless oral prayer to Jesus Christ, and I felt absolute peace in my soul. During sleep I often dreamed that I was saying the Prayer. And during the day if I happened to meet anyone, all men without exception were as dear to me as if they had been my nearest relations. But I did not concern myself with them much. All my ideas were quite calmed of their own accord. I thought of nothing whatever but my Prayer, my mind tended to listen to it, and my heart began of itself to feel at times a certain warmth and pleasure. If I happened to go to church the lengthy service of the monastery seemed short to me, and no longer wearied me as it had in time past. My lonely hut seemed like a splendid palace, and I knew not how to thank God for having sent to me, a lost sinner, so wholesome a guide and master.

But I was not long to enjoy the teaching of my dear *starets*, who was so full of divine wisdom. He died at the end of the summer. Weeping freely I bade him farewell, and thanked him for the fatherly teaching he had given my wretched self, and as a blessing and a keepsake I begged for the rosary with which he said his prayers.

And so I was left alone. Summer came to an end and the kitchen garden was cleared. I had no longer any-where to live. My peasant sent me away, giving me by way of wages two roubles, and filling up my bag with dried bread for my journey. Again I started off on my wanderings. But now I did not walk along as before, filled with care. The calling upon the Name of Jesus Christ gladdened my way. Everybody was kind to me, it was as though everyone loved me.

Then it occurred to me to wonder what I was to do with the money I had earned by my care of the kitchen garden. What good was it to me? Yet stay! I no longer had a *starets*, there was no one to go on teaching me. Why not buy *The Philokalia* and continue to learn from it more about interior prayer?

I crossed myself and set off with my Prayer. I came to a large town, where I asked for the book in all the shops. In the end I found it, but they asked me three roubles for it, and I had only two. I bargained for a long time, but the shopkeeper would not budge an inch. Finally he said, " Go to this church near by, and speak to the churchwarden. He has a book like that, but it's a very old copy. Perhaps he will let you have it for two roubles." I went, and sure enough I found and bought for my two roubles a worn and old copy of *The Philokalia*. I was delighted with it. I mended my book as much as I could, I made a cover for it with a piece of cloth, and put it into my breast pocket with my Bible.

And that is how I go about now, and ceaselessly repeat the Prayer of Jesus, which is more precious and sweet to me than anything in the world. At times I do as much as forty-three or four miles a day, and do not feel that I am walking at all. I am aware only of the fact that

I am saying my Prayer. When the bitter cold pierces me, I begin to say my Prayer more earnestly and I quickly get warm all over. When hunger begins to overcome me, I call more often on the Name of Jesus, and I forget my wish for food. When I fall ill and get rheumatism in my back and legs, I fix my thoughts on the Prayer and do not notice the pain. If anyone harms me I have only to think, " How sweet is the Prayer of Jesus ! " and the injury and the anger alike pass away and I forget it all. I have become a sort of half-conscious person. I have no cares and no interests. The fussy business of the world I would not give a glance to. The one thing I wish for is to be alone, and all by myself to pray, to pray without ceasing ; and doing this, I am filled with joy. God knows what is happening to me ! Of course, all this is sensuous, or as my departed *starets* said, an artificial state which follows naturally upon routine. But because of my unworthiness and stupidity I dare not venture yet to go on further, and learn and make my own, spiritual prayer within the depths of my heart. I await God's time. And in the meanwhile I rest my hope on the prayers of my departed *starets*. Thus, although I have not yet reached that ceaseless spiritual prayer which is self-acting in the heart, yet I thank God I do now understand the meaning of those words I heard in the Epistle— " *Pray without ceasing.*"

2

I WANDERED about for a long time in different districts, having for my fellow-traveller the Prayer of Jesus, which heartened and consoled me in all my journeys, in all my meetings with other people and in all the happenings of travel.

But I came to feel at last that it would be better for me to stay in some one place, in order to be alone more often, so as to be able to keep by myself and study *The Philokalia*. Although I read it whenever I found shelter for the night or rested during the day, yet I greatly wished to go more and more deeply into it, and with faith and heartfelt prayer to learn from it teaching about the truth for the salvation of my soul.

However, in spite of all my wishes, I could nowhere find any work that I was able to do, for I had lost the use of my left arm when quite a child. Seeing that because of this I should not be able to get myself a fixed abode, I made up my mind to go into Siberia to the tomb of St. Innocent of Irkutsk. My idea was that in the forests and steppes of Siberia I should travel in greater silence and therefore in a way that was better for prayer and reading. And this journey I undertook, all the while saying my oral Prayer without stopping.

After no great lapse of time I had the feeling that the Prayer had, so to speak, by its own action passed from my lips to my heart. That is to say, it seemed as though my heart in its ordinary beating began to say the words of the Prayer within at each beat. Thus for example, *one*, " Lord," *two*, " Jesus," *three*, " Christ," and so on. I gave up saying the Prayer with my lips. I simply listened carefully to what my heart was saying. It seemed as though my eyes looked right down into it; and I dwelt upon the words of my departed *starets* when he was telling me about this joy. Then I felt something like a slight pain in my heart, and in my thoughts so great a love for Jesus Christ that I pictured myself, if only I could see Him, throwing myself at His feet and not letting them go from my embrace, kissing them tenderly, and thanking Him with tears for having of His love and grace allowed me to find so great a consolation in His Name, me, His unworthy and sinful creature! Further there came into my heart a gracious warmth which spread through my whole breast. This moved me to a still closer reading of *The Philokalia* in order to test my feelings, and to make a thorough study of the business of secret prayer in the heart. For without such testing I was afraid of falling a victim to the mere charm of it, or of taking natural effects for the effects of grace, and of giving way to pride at my quick learning of the Prayer. It was of this danger that I had heard my departed *starets* speak. For this reason I took to walking more by night, and chose to spend my days reading *The Philokalia* sitting down under a tree in the forest. Ah! what wisdom, such as I had never known before, was shown me by this reading! Giving myself up to it I felt a delight which till then I had never been able to imagine. It is true that many places were still beyond the grasp of my dull mind. But my prayer in the heart brought with it the clearing up of things I did not understand. Sometimes also, though very rarely, I saw my departed *starets* in a dream, and he threw light upon many things, and, most of all, guided my ignorant soul more and more towards humility.

In this blissful state I passed more than two months of the summer. For the most part I went through the forests and along by-paths. When I came to a village I asked only for a bag of dried bread and a handful of salt. I filled my bark jar with water, and so on for another sixty miles or so.

Towards the end of the summer temptation began to attack me, perhaps as a result of the sins on my wretched soul, perhaps as something needed in the spiritual life, perhaps as the best way of giving me teaching and experience. A clear case in point was the following. One day when I came out on to the main road as twilight was falling, two men with shaved heads who looked like a couple of soldiers, came up to me. They demanded money. When I told them that I had not a farthing on me, they would not believe me, and shouted insolently, " You're lying, pilgrims always pick up lots of money."

" What's the good of arguing with him ! " said one of them, and gave me such a blow on the head with his oak cudgel that I dropped senseless. I do not know whether I remained senseless long, but when I came to I found myself lying in the forest by the roadside robbed. My knapsack had gone, all that was left of it were the cords from which it hung, which they had cut. Thank God they had not stolen my passport, which I carried in my old fur cap so as to be able to show it as quickly as possible on demand. I got up weeping bitterly, not so much on account of the pain in my head as for the loss of my books, the Bible and *The Philokalia*, which were in the stolen knapsack.

Day and night I did not cease to weep and lament. Where was it now, my Bible which I had always carried with me, and which I had always read from my youth onwards? Where was my *Philokalia*, from which I had gained so much teaching and consolation? Oh unhappy me, to have lost the first and last treasures of my life before having had my fill of them! It would have been better to be killed outright than to live without this spiritual food. For I should never be able to replace the books now.

For two days I just dragged myself along, I was so crushed by the weight of my misfortune, and on the third I quite reached the end of my strength, and dropping down in the shelter of a bush I feel asleep. And then I had a dream. I was back at the monastery in the cell of my *starets* deploring my loss. The old man was trying to comfort me. He said, " Let this be a lesson to you in detachment from earthly things, for your better advance towards heaven. This has been allowed to happen to you to save you from falling into the mere enjoyment of spiritual things. God would have the Christian absolutely renounce all his desires and delights and attachments, and to submit himself entirely to His divine will. He orders every event for the help and salvation of man; *He willeth that all men should be saved*. Take courage then and believe that God *will with the temptation provide also a way of escape*. (1 Cor., x, 13.) Soon you will be rejoicing much more than you are now distressed." At these words I awoke, feeling my strength come back to me and my soul full of light and peace. "God's will be done," I said. I crossed myself, got up and went on my way. The Prayer again began to be active in my heart, as before, and for three days I went along in peace.

All at once I came upon a body of convicts with their military escort. When I came up to them I recognised the two men who had robbed me. They were in the outside file, and so I fell at their feet and earnestly begged them to tell me what they had done with my books. At first they paid no heed to me, but in the end one of them said, "If you will give us something we will tell you where your books are. Give us a rouble." I swore to them that even if I had to beg the rouble from someone for the love of God, I would certainly give it to them, and by way of pledge I offered them my passport. Then they told me that my books were in the wagons which followed the prisoners, among all the other stolen things they were found with.

"How can I get them?"

"Ask the officer in charge of us."

I hurried to the officer and told him the whole story.

"Can you really read the Bible?" he asked me.

"Yes," I answered, "not only can I read everything,

23

but what is more, I can write too. You will see a signature in the Bible which shows it is mine, and here is my passport showing the same name and surname."

He then told me that the rascals who had robbed me were deserters living in a mud hut in the forest and that they had plundered many people, but that a clever driver whose *troika* they had tried to steal had captured them the day before. "All right," he added, "I will give you your books back if they are there, but you come with us as far as our halting place for the night; it is only a little over two miles, then I need not stop the whole convoy and the wagons just for your sake." I agreed to this gladly, and as I walked along at his horse's side, we began to talk.

I saw that he was a kindly and honest fellow and no longer young. He asked me who I was, where I came from, and where I was going. I answered all his questions without hiding anything, and so we reached the house which marked the end of the day's march. He found my books and gave them back to me, saying, "Where are you going, now night has come on? Stay here and sleep in my ante-room." So I stayed.

Now that I had my books again, I was so glad that I did not know how to thank God. I clasped the books to my breast and held them there so long that my hands got quite numbed. I shed tears of joy, and my heart beat with delight. The officer watched me and said, "You must love reading your Bible very much!" But such was my joy that I could not answer him, I could only weep. Then he went on to say, "I also read the

Gospel regularly every day, brother." He produced a small copy of the Gospels, printed in Kiev and bound in silver, saying, " Sit down, and I will tell you how it came about."

" Hullo there, let us have some supper," he shouted.

We drew up to the table and the officer began his story.

" Ever since I was a young man I have been with the army in the field and not on garrison service. I knew my job, and my superior officers liked me for a conscientious second-lieutenant. Still, I was young, and so were my friends. Unhappily I took to drink, and drunkenness became a regular passion with me. So long as I kept away from drink, I was a good officer, but when I gave way to it, I was no good for anything for six weeks at a time. They bore with me for a long while, but the end of it was that after being thoroughly rude while drunk to my commanding officer, I was cashiered and transferred to a garrison as a private soldier for three years. I was threatened with a still more severe punishment if I did not give up drinking and mend my ways. Even in this miserable state of affairs, however much I tried, I could not regain my self-control, nor cure myself. I found it impossible to get rid of my passion for drink, and it was decided to send me to a disciplinary corps. When I was informed of this I was at my wits' end. I was in barracks occupied with my wretched thoughts when there arrived a monk who was going round collecting for a church. We each of us gave him what we could.

" He came up to me and asked me why I was so

unhappy, and I talked to him and told him my troubles. He sympathised with me and said, ' The same thing happened to my own brother, and what do you think helped him ? His spiritual father gave him a copy of the Gospels with strict orders to read a chapter without a moment's delay every time he felt a longing for wine coming over him. If the desire continued he was to read a second chapter, and so on. That is what my brother did, and at the end of a very short time his drunkenness came to an end. It is now fifteen years since he touched a drop of alcohol. You do the same and you will see how that will help you. I have a copy of the Gospels which you must let me bring you.'

" I listened to him, and then I said, ' How can your Gospels help me since all efforts of my own and all the medical treatment have failed to stop me drinking ? ' I talked in that way because I had as yet never been in the habit of reading the Gospels. ' Don't say that,' replied the monk, ' I assure you that it will be a help.' As a matter of fact, the next day he brought me this very copy. I opened it, took a glance, and said, ' I cannot accept it, I am not used to Church Slavonic and don't understand it.' But the monk went on to assure me that in the very words of the Gospel there lay a gracious power, for in them was written what God Himself had spoken. ' It does not matter very much if at first you do not understand, go on reading diligently. A monk once said, " If you do not understand the Word of God, the devils understand what you are reading, and tremble," and your drunkenness is certainly the work of devils. And here is another thing I will tell you. St. John Chrysostom writes that even a room in which a copy of the Gospels is kept, holds the spirits of darkness at bay, and becomes an unpromising field for their wiles.'

" I forget what I gave the monk. But I bought his book of the Gospels, put it away in a trunk with my other things and forgot it. Some while afterwards a bout of drunkenness threatened me. An irresistible desire for drink drove me hurriedly to open my trunk to get some money and rush off to the public-house. But the first thing my eyes fell on was the copy of the Gospels, and all that the monk had said came back vividly to my mind. I opened the book and began to read the first chapter of St. Matthew. I got to the end of it without understanding a word. Still I remembered that the monk had said, ' No matter if you do not understand, go on reading diligently.' ' Come,' said I, ' I must read the second chapter.' I did so and began to understand a little. So I started on the third chapter and then the barracks bell began to ring ; everyone had to go to bed, no one was allowed to go out, and I had to stay where I was. When I got up in the morning I was just on the point of going out to get some wine when I suddently thought—supposing I were to read another chapter ? What would be the result ? I read it and I did not go to the public-house. Again I felt the craving, and again I read a chapter. I felt a certain amount of relief. This encouraged me, and from that time on, whenever I felt the need of drink, I used to read a chapter of the Gospels. What is more, as time went on things got better and better, and by the time I had finished all four Gospels my drunkenness was absolutely a thing of the past, and I felt nothing but disgust for it. It is just twenty years now since I drank a drop of alcohol.

" Everybody was astonished at the change brought about in me. Some three years later my commission was restored to me. In due course I was promoted, and finally got my majority. I married; I am blessed with a good wife, we have made a position for ourselves, and so, thank God, we go on living our life. As far as we can, we help the poor and give hospitality to pilgrims. Why, now I have a son who is an officer and a first-rate fellow. And mark this—since the time when I was cured of drunkenness, I have lived under a vow to read the Gospels every single day of my life, one whole Gospel in every twenty-four hours, and I let nothing whatever hinder me. I do this still. If I am exceedingly pressed with business, and unusually tired, I lie down and get my wife or my son to read the whole of one of the Evangelists to me, and so avoid breaking my rule. By way of thanksgiving and for the glory of God I have had this book of the Gospels mounted in pure silver, and I always carry it in my breast pocket."

I listened with great joy to this story of his. " I also have come across a case of the same sort," I told him. " At the factory in our village there was a craftsman, very skilful at his job, and a good, kindly fellow. Unhappily, however, he also drank, and very often at that. A certain God-fearing man advised him when the desire for drink seized him, to repeat the Prayer of Jesus thirty-three times in honour of the Holy Trinity, and in memory of the thirty-three years of the earthly life of Jesus Christ. He took his advice and started to carry it out, and very soon he quite gave up drinking. And, what is more, three years later he went into a monastery."

" And which is the best," he asked, " the Prayer of Jesus, or the Gospels ? "

" It's all one and the same thing," I answered. " What the Gospel is, that the Prayer of Jesus is also, for the Divine Name of Jesus Christ holds in itself the whole gospel truth. The holy Fathers say that the Prayer of Jesus is a summary of the Gospels."

After our talk we said prayers, and the Major began to read the Gospel of St. Mark from the beginning, and I listened and said the Prayer in my heart. At two o'clock in the morning he came to the end of the Gospel, and we parted and went to bed.

As usual I got up early in the morning. Everyone was still asleep. As soon as it began to get light, I eagerly seized my beloved *Philokalia*. With what gladness I opened it ! I might have been getting a glimpse of my own father coming back from a far country, or of a friend risen from the dead. I kissed it, and thanked God for giving it me back again. I began at once to read Theolept of Philadelphia, in the second part of the book. His teaching surprised me when he lays down that one and the same person at one and the same time should do three quite different things. " Seated at table," he says, " supply your body with food, your ear with reading and your mind with prayer." But the memory

29

of the very happy evening the day before really gave me from my own experience the meaning of this thought. And here also the secret was revealed to me that the mind and the heart are not one and the same thing.

As soon as the Major rose I went to thank him for his kindness and to say good-bye. He gave me tea and a rouble and bade me farewell. I set off again feeling very happy. I had gone over half a mile when I remembered I had promised the soldiers a rouble, and that now this rouble had come to me in a quite unlooked-for way. Should I give it to them or not? At first I thought: they beat you and they robbed you, moreover this money will be of no use to them whatever, since they are under arrest. But afterwards other thoughts came to me. Remember it is written in the Bible, " *If thine enemy hunger feed him,*" and Jesus Christ himself said, " *Love your enemies,*" " *And if any man will take away thy coat let him have thy cloak also.*" That settled it for me. I went back and just as I got to the house all the convicts came out to start on the next stage of their march. I went quickly up to my two soldiers, I handed them my rouble and said, " Repent and pray! Jesus Christ loves men, He will not forsake you." And with that I left them and went on my way.

After doing some thirty miles along the main road I thought I would take a by-path so that I might be more by myself and read more quietly. For a long while I walked through the heart of the forest, and but rarely came upon a village. At times I passed almost the whole day sitting under the trees and carefully reading *The*

Philokalia, from which I gained a surprising amount of knowledge. My heart kindled with desire for union with God by means of interior prayer, and I was eager to learn it under the guidance and control of my book. At the same time I felt sad that I had no dwelling where I could give myself up quietly to reading all the while. During this time I read my Bible also, and I felt that I began to understand it more clearly than before, when I had failed to understand many things in it and had often been a prey to doubts. The holy Fathers were right when they said that *The Philokalia* is a key to the mysteries of Holy Scripture. With the help it gave me I began to some extent to understand the hidden meaning of the Word of God. I began to see the meaning of such sayings as—" The inner secret man of the heart," " true prayer worships in the spirit," " the kingdom is within us," " the intercession of the Holy Spirit with groanings that cannot be uttered," " abide in me," " give me thy heart," " to put on Christ," " the betrothal of the Spirit to our hearts," the cry from the depths of the heart, " Abba, Father," and so on. And when with all this in mind I prayed with my heart, everything around me seemed delightful and marvellous. The trees, the grass, the birds, the earth, the air, the light seemed to be telling me that they existed for man's sake, that they witnessed to the love of God for man, that everything proved the love of God for man, that all things prayed to God and sang His praise.

Thus it was that I came to understand what *The Philokalia* calls " the knowledge of the speech of all creatures," and I saw the means by which converse could be held with God's creatures.

In this way I wandered about for a long while, coming at length to so lonely a district that for three days I came upon no village at all. My supply of dried bread was used up, and I began to be very much cast down at the thought I might die of hunger. I began to pray my hardest in the depths of my heart. All my fears went, and I entrusted myself to the will of God. My peace of mind came back to me, and I was in good spirits again. When I had gone a little further along the road, which here skirted a huge forest, I caught sight of a dog which came out of it and ran along in front of me. I called it, and it came up to me with a great show of friendliness. I was glad, and I thought, Here is another case of God's goodness! No doubt there is a flock grazing in the forest and this dog belongs to the shepherd. Or perhaps somebody is shooting in the neighbourhood. Whichever it is I shall be able to beg a piece of bread if nothing more, for I have eaten nothing for twenty-four hours. Or at least I shall be able to find out where the nearest village is.

After jumping around me for some little time and seeing that I was not going to give him anything, the dog trotted back into the forest along the narrow footpath by which he had come out. I followed, and a few hundred yards further on, looking between the trees, I saw him run into a hole, from which he looked out and began to bark. At the same time a thin and pale middle-aged peasant came into view from behind a great tree.

He asked me where I came from, and for my part I wanted to know how he came to be there, and so we started a friendly talk.

He took me into his mud hut and told me that he was a forester and that he looked after this particular wood, which had been sold for felling. He set bread and salt before me, and we began to talk. " How I envy you," said I, " being able to live so nicely alone in this quiet instead of being like me ! I wander from place to place and rub along with all sorts of people."

" You can stop here too, if you like," he answered. " The old forester's hut is quite near here. It is half ruined, but still quite fit to live in in summer. I suppose you have your passport. As far as bread goes, we shall always have plenty of that, it is brought to me every week from my village. This spring here never dries up. For my part, brother, I have eaten nothing but bread and have drunk nothing but water for the last ten years. This is how things stand. When autumn comes and the peasants have ended their work on the land, some two hundred workmen will be coming to cut down this wood. Then I shall have no further business here, and you will not be allowed to stay either."

As I listened to all this I all but fell at his feet, I felt so pleased. I did not know how to thank God for such goodness. In this unlooked-for way my greatest wish was to be granted me. There were still over four months before next autumn ; during all that time I could enjoy the silence and peace needed for a close reading of *The Philokalia* in order to study and learn ceaseless prayer in the heart. So I very gladly stayed there, to live during that time in the hut he showed me.

I talked further with this simple brother who gave me shelter, and he told me about his life and his ideas. " I had quite a good position in the life of our village," said he. " I had a workshop where I dyed fustian and linen, and I lived comfortably enough, though not without sin. I often cheated in business, I was a false swearer, I was abusive, I used to drink and quarrel. In our village there was an old *dyachok* ³ who had a very old book on the Last Judgment. He used to go from house to house and read from it, and he was paid something for doing so. He came to me too. Give him threepence and a glass of wine into the bargain and he would go on reading all night till cock crow. There I would sit at my work and listen while he read about the torments that await us in Hell. I heard how the living will be changed and the dead raised; how God will come down to judge the world; how the angels will sound the trumpets; I heard of the fire and pitch, and of the worm which will devour sinners. One day as I listened I was seized with horror, and I said to myself : What if these torments come upon me ! I will set to work to save my soul. It may be that by prayer I can avoid the results of my sins. I thought about this for a long time. Then I gave up my work, sold my house, and as I was alone in the world, I got a place as forester here and all I ask of my *mir* ⁴ is bread, clothes and some candles for my prayers. I have been living like this for over ten years now. I eat only once a day and then nothing but bread and water. I get up at cock crow, make my devotions and say my prayers before the holy icons with seven candles burning. When I make my rounds in the forest during the day, I wear iron chains weighing sixty pounds next my skin. I never grumble, drink neither wine nor beer, I never quarrel with anybody at all, and I have had nothing to do with women and girls all my life. At first this sort of life pleased me, but lately other thoughts have come into my mind, and I cannot get away from them. God only knows if I shall be able to pray my sins away in this fashion, and it's a hard life. And is everything written in that book true? How can a dead man rise again? Supposing he has been dead over a hundred years and not even his ashes are left? Who knows if there is really a Hell or not? What more is known of a man after he dies and rots? Perhaps the book was written by priests and masters to make us poor fools afraid and keep us quiet. What if we plague ourselves for nothing and give up all our pleasure in vain? Suppose there is no such thing as another life, what then? Isn't it better to enjoy one's earthly life, and take it easily and happily? Ideas of this kind often worry me, and I don't know but what I shall not some day go back to my old work."

I heard him with pity. They say, I thought, that it is only the learned and the clever who are free thinkers and believe in nothing! Yet here is one of ourselves, even a simple peasant, a prey to such unbelief. The kingdom of darkness throws open its gates to everyone, it seems, and maybe attacks the simple-minded most easily. Therefore one must learn wisdom and strengthen oneself with the Word of God as much as possible against the enemy of the soul.

So with the object of helping this brother and doing all I could to strengthen his faith, I took *The Philokalia* out of my knapsack. Turning to the 109th chapter of Isikhi, I read it to him. I set out to prove to him the uselessness and vanity of avoiding sin merely from fear of the tortures of Hell, I told him that the soul could be freed from sinful thoughts only by guarding the mind and cleansing the heart, and that this could be done by interior prayer. I added that according to the holy Fathers, one who performs saving works simply from the fear of Hell follows the way of bondage, and he who does the same just in order to be rewarded with the Kingdom of Heaven follows the path of a bargainer with God. The one they call a slave, the other a hireling. But God wants us to come to Him as sons to their Father, He wants us to behave ourselves honourably from love for Him and zeal for His service, He wants us to find our happiness in uniting ourselves with Him in a saving union of mind and heart.

" However much you spend yourself on treating your body hardly," I said, " you will never find peace of mind that way, and unless you have God in your mind and the ceaseless Prayer of Jesus in your heart, you will always be likely to fall back into sin for the very slightest reason. Set to work, my brother, upon the ceaseless saying of the Prayer of Jesus. You have such a good chance of doing so here in this lonely place, and in a short while you will see the gain of it. No godless thoughts will then be able to get at you, and the true faith and love for Jesus Christ will be shown to you. You will then understand how the dead will be raised, and you will see the Last Judgment in its true light. The Prayer will make you feel such lightness and such bliss in your heart, that you will be astonished at it yourself, and your wholesome way of life will be neither dull nor troublesome to you."

Then I went on to explain to him as well as I could how to begin, and how to go on ceaselessly with the Prayer of Jesus, and how the Word of God and the writings of the holy Fathers teach us about it. He agreed with it all and seemed to me to be calmer.

Then I left him and shut myself up in the hut which he had shown me. Ah! how delighted I was, how calmly happy when I crossed the threshold of that lonely retreat, or rather, that tomb! It seemed to me like a magnificent palace filled with every consolation and delight. With tears of rapture I gave thanks to God and said to myself, Here in this peace and quietude I must seriously set to work at my task and beseech God to give me light. So I started by reading through *The Philokalia* again with great care, from beginning to end. Before long I had read the whole of it, and I saw how much wisdom, holiness and depth of insight there was in this book. Still, so many matters were dealt with in it, and it contained such a lot of lessons from the holy Fathers, that I could not very well grasp it all, and take in as a single whole what was said about interior prayer. And this was what I chiefly wanted to know, so as to learn from it how to practise ceaseless self-acting prayer in the heart.

This was my great desire, following the divine command in the Apostle's words, " *Covet earnestly the best gifts*," and again, " *Quench not the Spirit*." I thought over the matter for a long time. What was to be done? My mind and my understanding were not equal to the task, and there was no one to explain. I made up my mind to besiege God with prayer. Maybe He would make me understand somehow. For twenty-four hours I did nothing but pray without stopping for a single moment. At last my thoughts were calmed, and I fell asleep. And then I dreamed that I was in my departed *starets'* cell and that he was explaining *The Philokalia* to me. " The holy book is full of profound wisdom," he was saying. " It is a secret treasury of the meaning of the hidden judgments of God. It is not everywhere and to everyone that it is accessible, but it does give to each such guidance as he needs, to the wise, wise guidance, to the simple-minded, simple guidance. That is why you simple folk should not read the chapters one after the other as they are arranged in the book. That order is for those who are instructed in theology. Those who are uninstructed, but who nevertheless desire to learn interior prayer from this book, should take things in this order. (1) First of all read through the book of Nicephorus the monk (in part 2), then (2) the whole book of Gregory of Sinai, except the short chapters, (3) Simeon the New Theologian on the Three Forms of Prayer and his discourse on Faith, and after that (4) the book of Callistus and Ignatius. In these Fathers there are full directions and teaching on interior prayer of the heart, in a form which everyone can understand.

" And if, in addition, you want to find a very understandable instruction on prayer, turn to part 4 and find the summarised pattern of prayer by the most holy Callistus, Patriarch of Constantinople."

In my dream I held the book in my hands and began to look for this passage, but I was quite unable to find it. Then he turned over a few pages himself and said, " Here it is, I will mark it for you." He picked up a piece of charcoal from the ground and made a mark in the margin, against the passage he had found. I listened to him with care, and tried to fix in my mind everything he said, word for word. When I woke up it was still dark. I lay still and in thought went over my dream and all that my *starets* had said to me. " God knows," thought I, " whether it is really the spirit of my departed *starets* that I have seen, or whether it is only the outcome of my own thoughts, because they are so often taken up with *The Philokalia* and my *starets*." With this doubt in my mind I got up, for day was beginning to break; and what did I see? There on the stone which served as a table in my hut lay the book open at the very page which my *starets* had pointed out to me, and in the margin, a charcoal mark just as in my dream! Even the piece of charcoal itself was lying beside the book! I looked in astonishment, for I remembered clearly that the book was not there the evening before, that it had been put, shut, under my pillow, and also I was quite certain that before there had been nothing where now I saw the charcoal mark.

It was this which made me sure of the truth of my dream, and that my revered master of blessed memory was pleasing to God. I set about reading *The Philokalia* in the exact order he had bidden. I read it once, and again a second time, and this reading kindled in my soul a zealous desire to make what I had read a matter of practical experience. I saw clearly what interior prayer means, how it is to be reached, what the fruits of it are, how it filled one's heart and soul with delight, and how one could tell whether that delight came from God, from nature or from temptation.

So I began by searching out my heart in the way Simeon the New Theologian teaches. With my eyes shut I gazed in thought, *i.e.*, in imagination, upon my heart. I tried to picture it there in the left side of my breast and to listen carefully to its beating. I started doing this several times a day, for half an hour at a time, and at first I felt nothing but a sense of darkness. But little by little after a fairly short time I was able to picture my heart and to note its movement, and further with the help of my breathing I could put into it and draw from it the Prayer of Jesus in the manner taught by the saints, Gregory of Sinai, Callistus and Ignatius. When drawing the air in I looked in spirit into my heart and said, " Lord Jesus Christ," and when breathing out again, I said, " Have mercy on me." I did this at first for an hour at a time, then for two hours, then for as long as I could, and in the end almost all day long. If any difficulty arose, if sloth or doubt came upon me, I hastened to take up *The Philokalia* and read again those parts which dealt with the work of the heart, and then once more I felt ardour and zeal for the Prayer.

When about three weeks had passed I felt a pain in my heart, and then a most delightful warmth, as well as consolation and peace. This aroused me still more and spurred me on more and more to give great care to the saying of the Prayer so that all my thoughts were taken up with it and I felt a very great joy. From this time I began to have from time to time a number of different feelings in my heart and mind. Sometimes my heart would feel as though it were bubbling with joy, such lightness, freedom and consolation were in it. Sometimes I felt a burning love for Jesus Christ and for all God's creatures. Sometimes my eyes brimmed over with tears of thankfulness to God, who was so merciful to me, a wretched sinner. Sometimes my understanding, which had been so stupid before, was given so much light that I could easily grasp and dwell upon matters of which up to now I had not been able even to think at all. Sometimes that sense of a warm gladness in my heart spread throughout my whole being and I was deeply moved as the fact of the presence of God everywhere was brought home to me. Sometimes by calling upon the Name of Jesus I was overwhelmed with bliss, and now I knew the meaning of the words " *The Kingdom of God is within you.* "

From having all these and other like feelings I noted that interior prayer bears fruit in three ways : in the

Spirit, in the feelings, and in revelations. In the first, for instance, is the sweetness of the love of God, inward peace, gladness of mind, purity of thought, and the sweet remembrance of God. In the second, the pleasant warmth of the heart, fulness of delight in all one's limbs, the joyous "bubbling" in the heart, lightness and courage, the joy of living, power not to feel sickness and sorrow. And in the last, light given to the mind, understanding of Holy Scripture, knowledge of the speech of created things, freedom from fuss and vanity, knowledge of the joy of the inner life, and finally certainty of the nearness of God and of His love for us.

After spending five months in this lonely life of prayer and such happiness as this, I grew so used to the Prayer that I went on with it all the time. In the end I felt it going on of its own accord within my mind and in the depths of my heart, without any urging on my part. Not only when I was awake, but even during sleep just the same thing went on. Nothing broke into it and it never stopped even for a single moment, whatever I might be doing. My soul was always giving thanks to God and my heart melted away with unceasing happiness.

The time came for the wood to be felled. People began to come along in crowds, and I had to leave my quiet dwelling. I thanked the forester, said some prayers, kissed the bit of the earth which God had deigned to give me, unworthy of His mercy as I was, shouldered my bag of books, and set off.

For a very long while I wandered about in different places until I reached Irkutsk. The self-acting Prayer in my heart was a comfort and consolation all the way ; whatever I met with it never ceased to gladden me, though it did so to different degrees at different times. Wherever I was, whatever I did or gave myself up to, it never hindered things, nor was hindered by them. If I am working at anything the Prayer goes on by itself in my heart, and the work gets on faster. If I am listening carefully to anything, or reading, the Prayer never stops, at one and the same time I am aware of both just as if I were made into two people, or as if there were two souls in my one body. Lord! what a mysterious thing man is! " *How manifold are thy works, O Lord! In wisdom hast Thou made them all.*"

All sorts of things and many strange adventures happened to me as I went on my way. If I were to start telling them all, I should not end in twenty-four hours. Thus for example, one winter evening as I was going alone through the forest towards a village which I could see about a mile away, and where I was to spend the night, a great wolf suddenly came in sight and made for me. I had in my hand my *starets'* woollen rosary, which I always carried with me. I struck at the animal with that. Well, the rosary was torn out of my hands and got twisted round the wolf's neck. He leapt away from me, but in jumping through a thorn bush he got his hind paws caught. The rosary also caught on a bough of a dead tree and he began dashing himself about, but he could not free himself because the rosary was tightening round his throat. I crossed myself in faith and went forward to free him, chiefly because I was afraid that if

43

he tore my rosary away and ran off with it, I should lose
my precious rosary. And sure enough, as soon as I got
hold of the rosary the wolf snapped it and fled without
leaving a trace. I thanked God, with my blessed *starets*
in mind, and I came safe and sound to the village, where
I asked for a night's lodging at an inn.

I went into the house. Two men, one of them old and
the other middle-aged and heavily built, were sitting at
a table in a corner drinking tea. They looked as though
they were not just simple folk, and I asked the peasant
who was with their horses who they were. He told me
that the elder of the two was a teacher at an elementary
school, and the other the clerk of the County Court.
They were both people of the better class. He was
driving them to a fair about a dozen miles away. After
sitting a while, I asked the hostess to lend me a needle
and thread, came over into the candle-light, and set
about mending my broken rosary.

The clerk watched what I was doing and said, " I
suppose you have been praying so hard that your rosary
broke ? "

" It was not I who broke it," I answered, " it was a
wolf."

" What ! A wolf ? Do wolves say their prayers,
too ? " said he jokingly.

I told them all that had happened, and how precious
the rosary was to me. The clerk laughed again, saying,
" Miracles are always happening with you sham saints !
What was there sacred about a thing like that ? The
simple fact was that you brandished something at the

wolf and he was frightened and went off. Of course, dogs and wolves take fright at the gesture of throwing, and getting caught on to a tree is common enough. That sort of thing very often happens. Where is the miracle ? "

But the old man answered him thus : " Do not jump to conclusions like that, sir. You miss the deeper aspects of the incident. For my part I see in this peasant's story the mystery of nature, both sensuous and spiritual."

" How's that ? " asked the clerk.

" Well, like this. Although you have not received the highest education, you have, of course, learned the sacred history of the Old and New Testaments, as summarised in the questions and answers used at school. You remember that when our father Adam was still in a state of holy innocence all the animals were obedient to him, they approached him in fear and received from him their names. The old man to whom this rosary belonged was a saint. Now what is the meaning of sanctity ? For the sinner it means nothing else than a return through effort and discipline to the state of innocence of the first man. When the soul is made holy the body becomes holy also. The rosary had always been in the hands of a sanctified person ; the effect of the contact of his hands and the exhalation of his body was to inoculate it with holy power—the power of the first man's innocence. That is the mystery of spiritual nature ! All animals in natural succession down to the present time have experienced this power, and they experience it through smelling, for in all animals the

45

nose is the chief organ of sensation. That is the mystery of sensuous nature ! "

" You learned people go on about strength and wisdom," said the clerk, " but we take things more simply. Fill up a glass of vodka and tip it off ; that will give you strength enough." And he went over to the cupboard.

" That's your business," said the schoolmaster, " but please leave learning to us ! "

I liked the way he spoke, and I came up closer to him and said, " May I venture, Father, to tell you a little more about my *starets* ? " And so I told him about the appearance of my *starets* while I was asleep, the teaching he had given me, and the charcoal mark which he had made in *The Philokalia*. He listened with care to what I told him, but the clerk, who lay stretched out on a bench, muttered, " It's true enough you can lose your wits through reading the Bible too much. That's what it is ! Do you suppose a bogy man comes and marks your books at night ? You simply let the book drop on the ground yourself while you were asleep, and some soot made a dirty mark on it. There's your miracle ! Eh, you tricksters, I've come across plenty of your kidney ! "

Muttering this sort of thing, the clerk rolled over with his face to the wall and went to sleep. So I turned to the schoolmaster, saying, " If I may, I will show you the actual book. Look, it is really marked, not just dirtied with soot." I took it out of my knapsack and showed him. " What surprises me," said I, " is how a spirit without a body could have picked up a piece of charcoal and written with it." He looked at the mark and said,. "This also is a spiritual mystery. I will explain it to you. Look here now, when spirits appear in a bodily form to a living person, they compose themselves a body which can be felt, from the air and the world-stuff, and later on give back to the elements again what they had borrowed from them. Just as the atmosphere possesses elasticity, a power to contract and expand, so the soul, clothed in it, can take up anything, and act, and write. But what is this book of yours? Let me have a look at it." He began to look at it and it opened at the sermons of St. Simeon the New Theologian. "Ah, this must be a theological work. I have never seen it before," he said.

"It is almost wholly made up," I told him, "of teaching on interior prayer of the heart in the Name of Jesus Christ. It is set forth here in full detail by twenty-five holy Fathers."

"Ah, I know something of interior prayer," he answered.

I bowed before him, down to the very ground, and begged him to speak to me about interior prayer.

"Well, it says in the New Testament that man and all creation '*are subject to vanity, not willingly,*' and sigh with effort and desire to enter into the liberty of the children of God. The mysterious sighing of creation, the innate aspiration of every soul towards God, that is exactly what interior prayer is. There is no need to learn it, it is innate in every one of us!"

"But what is one to do to find it in oneself, to feel it in one's heart, to acknowledge it by one's will, to take

47

it and feel the happiness and light of it, and so to reach salvation ? " I asked.

" I don't know whether there is anything on the subject in theological books," said he.

" Well, here it is. It is all explained here," I answered, showing him my book again. The schoolmaster noted the title and said he would certainly have one sent from Tobolsk and study it. After that we went our different ways. I thanked God for this talk with the schoolmaster, and prayed that God would so order things that the clerk also might read *The Philokalia*, even if only once, and let him find salvation through it.

Another time—it was in spring—I passed through a village where I stayed with the priest. He was a worthy man, living alone, and I spent three days with him. Having watched me for that length of time he said to me, " Stay here. I will pay you something. I need a trustworthy man ; as you see, we are starting to build a stone church here near the old wooden chapel, and I have been looking for some honest person to keep an eye on the workmen and stay in the chapel in charge of the offerings for the building fund. It is exactly the thing for you, and would just suit your way of life. You will be alone in the chapel and say your prayers. There is a quiet little room for a verger there. Please stay, at any rate until the building is finished."

For a long while I refused, but in the end I had to yield to the good priest's begging, and I stayed there till the autumn, taking up my abode in the chapel. At first I found it quiet and apt for prayer, although a great many people came to the chapel, especially on holidays, some to say their prayers, some because they were bored, and others again with the idea of pilfering from the collection plate. I read my Bible and my *Philokalia* every evening, and some of them saw this and started talking to me about it or asked me to read aloud.

After a while I noticed that a young village girl often came to the chapel, and spent a long while in prayer. Listening to her whisperings, I found that the prayers she was saying were some of them strange to me, and others the usual prayers in a garbled form. I asked her where she learned such things, and she told me it was from her mother, who was a churchwoman, but that her father belonged to a sect which had no priesthood. Feeling sorry for her, I advised her to read her prayers in the right form as given by the tradition of Holy Church. Then I taught her the right wording of the Lord's Prayer and of the Hail Mary, and finally I advised her to say the Prayer of Jesus as often as she could, for that brought one nearer to God than any other prayer. The girl took note of what I said and set about it quite simply. And what happened? A short time afterwards she told me that she was so used to the Prayer that she felt it draw her all the time, that she used it as much as she could, that she enjoyed the Prayer at the time, and that afterwards she was filled with gladness and a wish to begin using it again. I was glad of this, and advised her to go on with it more and more.

Summer was drawing to a close. Many visitors to the chapel came to see me also, not only to be read to and to ask for advice, but with all sorts of worldly troubles, and even to ask about things they had mislaid or lost. Some of them seemed to take me for a wizard. The girl I spoke about also came to me one day in a state of great distress and worry, not knowing what to do. Her father wanted to make her marry a man of his own religion, and they were to be married not by a priest but by a mere peasant belonging to the same sect. " How could that be a lawful marriage, wouldn't it be the same thing as fornication ? " cried the girl. She had made up her mind to run away somewhere or other.

" But," said I, " where to ? They would be sure to find you again. They will look everywhere, and you won't be able to hide anywhere from them. You had better pray earnestly to God to turn your father from his purpose and to guard your soul from sin and heresy. That is a much sounder plan than running away."

Thus time passed away, and all this noise and fuss began to be more than I could bear, and at last at the end of summer I made up my mind to leave the chapel and go on with my pilgrimage as before. I told the priest what was in my mind, saying, " You know my plans, Father, I must have quiet for prayer, and here it is very disturbing and bad for me, and I have spent the whole summer here. Now let me go, and give your blessing on my lonely journey."

But the priest did not want to let me go, and tried to get me to stay. " What is there to hinder your praying here ? Your work is nothing to speak of, beyond stopping in the chapel. You have your daily bread.

Say your prayers then all day and all night if you like, and live with God. You are useful here, you don't go in for silly gossip with the people who come here, you are a source of profit to the church. All that is worth more in God's sight than your prayers all by yourself. Why do you always want to be alone ? Common prayer is pleasanter. God did not create man to think of himself only, but that men should help each other and lead each other along the path to salvation, each according to his strength. Think of the saints and the Fathers of the Church ! They bustled about day and night, they cared for the needs of the Church, they used to preach all over the place. They didn't sit down alone and hide themselves from people."

" Everyone has his own gift from God," I answered. " There have been many preachers, Father, but there have also been many hermits. Everyone does what he can, as he sees his own line, with the thought that God Himself shows him the way of his salvation. How do you get over the fact that many of the saints gave up their positions as bishops or priests or the rule of a monastery and went into the desert to get away from the fuss which comes from living with other people ? St. Isaac the Syrian, for instance, fled from the flock whose bishop he was, and the venerable Athanasius of Athos left his large monastery just because to them these places were a source of temptation, and they sincerely believed Our Lord's saying, ' *What shall it profit a man if he gains the whole world and lose his own soul ?* ' "

" Ah, but they were saints," said the priest.

" And if," I answered, " the very saints took steps to guard themselves from the dangers of mingling with people, what else, I ask you, can a feeble sinner do ? "

So in the end I said good-bye to this good priest, and he, out of the love in his heart, set me on my way.

Some half-dozen miles further on, I stopped for the night at a village. At the inn there I found a peasant hopelessly ill, and I advised those who were with him to see that he had the last sacraments. They agreed, and towards morning sent for the parish priest. I stayed there too, because I wanted to worship and pray in the presence of the Holy Gifts, and going out into the street, sat down on the *zavalina* [5] to wait for the priest to come. All at once I was astonished to see running towards me from the backyard the girl who used to pray in the chapel.

" What brings you here ? " I asked.

" They had fixed the day of my betrothal to the man I told you of, so I left them." And kneeling before me she went on, " Have pity on me : take me with you and put me into some convent or other. I don't want to be married, I want to live in a convent and say the Jesus Prayer. They will listen to you and take me."

" Goodness ! " I exclaimed, " and where am I to take you to ? I don't know a single convent in this neighbourhood. Besides, I can't take you anywhere without a passport. For one thing, you wouldn't be taken in anywhere, and for another it would be quite impossible for you to hide nowadays. You would be caught at once and sent home again, and punished as a tramp into the bargain. You had far better go home and say your prayers there. And if you don't want to marry, make out you are ill. The holy mother Clementa did that, and so did the venerable Marina when she took refuge in a men's convent. There are many other cases of the same thing. It is called a saving pretence."

While all this was happening and we sat talking the matter over we saw four men driving up the road with a pair of horses and coming straight towards us at a gallop. They seized the girl and put her in the cart, and one of them drove off with her. The other three tied my hands together and haled me back to the village where I had spent the summer. Their only reply to everything I said for myself was to shout, " We'll teach the little saint to seduce young girls ! "

That evening they brought me to the village court, put my feet in irons and lodged me in gaol to await my trial in the morning. The priest heard that I was in prison and came to see me. He brought me some supper and comforted me, saying that he would do what he could for me, and give his word as a spiritual father that I was not the sort of person they thought. After sitting with me for a while, he went away.

The magistrate came late in the evening, driving through the village on his way to somewhere else, and stopped at the deputy's house, where they told him what had happened. He bade the peasants come together, and had me brought to the house which was used as a court. We went in and stood waiting. In comes the magistrate, blustering, and sits down on the table with his hat on.

" Hi ! Epiphan," he shouts, " did the girl, this daughter of yours, run off with anything from your house ? "

" No, sir, nothing," was the answer.

" Has she been found out doing anything wrong with that fool there ? "

" No, sir."

" Well then, this is my decision and my judgment in the matter ; you deal with your daughter yourself, and as for this fellow we will teach him a lesson to-morrow and throw him out of the village, with strict orders never to show his face here again. So that's that."

So saying, he got down from the table and went off to bed, while I was taken back to gaol. Early in the morning two country policemen came, flogged me and drove me out of the village. I went off thanking God that He counted me worthy to suffer for His Name. This comforted me and gave still more warmth and glow to my ceaseless interior prayer. None of these things made me feel at all cast down. It was as though they happened to someone else, and I merely watched them. Even the flogging was within my power to bear. The Prayer brought sweetness into my heart, and made me unaware, so to speak, of everything else.

A mile or two further on I met the girl's mother, coming home from market with what she had bought. Seeing me, she told me that the son-in-law to be had withdrawn his suit. " You see, he is annoyed with Akulka for having run away from him." Then she gave me some bread and patties, and I went on my way.

The weather was fine and dry and I had no wish to

spend the night in a village. So when I came upon two fenced-in haystacks as I went through the forest that evening, I lay down beneath them for a night's lodging. I fell asleep and dreamed that I was walking along and reading a chapter of St. Anthony the Great from *The Philokalia*. Suddenly my *starets* overtook me and said, "Don't read that, read this," and pointed to these words in the 35th chapter of St. John Karpathisky, "A teacher submits at times to ignominy and endures pain for the sake of his spiritual children." And again he made me note in the 41st chapter, "Those who give themselves most earnestly to prayer, it is they who become the prey of terrible and violent temptations." Then he said, "Take courage and do not be downcast. Remember the Apostle's words, 'Greater is he that is in you than he that is in the world.' You see that you have now had experience of the truth that no temptation is beyond man's strength to resist, and that with the temptation God makes also a way of escape. Reliance upon this divine help has strengthened holy men of prayer and led them on to greater zeal and ardour. They not only devoted their own lives to ceaseless prayer, but also out of the love of their hearts revealed it and taught it to others as opportunity occurred. St. Gregory of Thessalonika speaks of this as follows, 'Not only should we ourselves in accordance with God's will pray unceasingly in the Name of Jesus Christ, but we are bound to reveal it and teach it to others, to everyone in general, religious and secular, learned and simple, men, women and children, and to inspire them all with zeal for prayer without ceasing.' In the same way the venerable Callistus Telicudes says, ' One ought not to keep thoughts about God (*i.e.*, interior prayer) and what is learned by contemplation, and the means of raising the soul on high, simply in one's own mind, but one should make notes of it, put it into writing for general use and with a loving motive.' And the Scriptures say in this connection, ' *Brother is helped by brother like a strong and lofty city* ' (Prov. xviii, 19). Only in this case it is above all things necessary to avoid self-praise and to take care that the seed of divine teaching is not sown to the wind.''

I woke up feeling great joy in my heart and strength in my soul, and I went on my way.

A long while after this something else happened which also I will tell you about if you like. One day—it was the 24th of March to be exact—I felt a very urgent wish to make my communion the next day—that is, on the Feast of the Annunciation of our Lady. I asked whether the church was far away, and was told it was about twenty miles. So I walked for the rest of that day and all the next night in order to get there in time for Mattins. The weather was as bad as it could be, it snowed and rained, there was a strong wind and it was very cold. On my way I had to cross a small stream, and just as I got to the middle the ice gave way under my feet and I was plunged into the water up to my waist. Drenched like this, I came to Mattins and stood through it, and also through the Liturgy which followed, and at which by God's grace I made my communion. In order to spend the day quietly and without spoiling my spiritual happiness, I begged the verger to allow me to stay in his little room until the next morning. I was more happy than I can tell all that day, and my heart was full of joy. I lay on the plank bed in that unheated room as though I were resting on Abraham's bosom. The Prayer was very active. The love of Jesus Christ and of the Mother of God seemed to surge into my heart in waves of sweetness and steep my soul in consolation and triumph. At nightfall I was seized with violent rheumatic pains in my legs, and that brought to my mind that they were soaking wet. I took no notice of it, and set my heart the more to my Prayer, so that I no longer felt the pain. In the morning when I wanted to get up I found that I could not move my legs. They were quite paralysed, and as feeble as bits of string. The verger dragged me down off the bed by main force. And so there I sat for two days without moving. On the third day the verger set about turning me out of his room, " For," said he, " supposing you die here, what a fuss there will be ! " With the greatest of difficulty I somehow or other crawled along on my arms and dragged myself to the steps of the church, and lay there. And there I stayed like that for a couple of days. The people who went by passed me without taking the slightest notice either of me or of my pleadings. In the end a peasant came up to me and sat down and talked. And after a while he asked, " What will you give me if I cure you ? I had just exactly the same thing once, so I know a medicine for it."

" I have nothing to give you," I answered.

" But what have you got in your bag ? "

" Only dried bread and some books."

" Well, what about working for me just for one summer, if I cure you ? "

" I can't do any work ; as you see, I have only the use of one arm, the other is almost entirely withered."

" Then what can you do ? "

" Nothing, beyond the fact that I can read and write."

" Ah ! write ! well, teach my little boy to write. He can read a little, and I want him to be able to write too. But it costs such a lot, they want twenty roubles to teach him."

I agreed to this, and with the verger's help he carried me away and put me in an old empty bathhouse in his backyard.

Then he set about curing me. And this was his method. He picked up from the floors, the yards, the cesspools, the best part of a bushel of various sorts of putrid bones, bones of cattle, of birds—all sorts. He washed them, broke them up small with a stone, and put them into a great earthen pot. This he covered with a lid which had a small hole in it, and placed upside down on an empty jar sunk in the ground. He smeared the upper pot with a thick coating of clay, and making a pile of wood round it, he set fire to this and kept it burning for more than twenty-four hours, saying as he fed the fire, " Now we'll get some tar from the bones." Next day, when he took the lower jar out of the ground, there had dripped into it through the hole in the lid of the other jar about a pint of thick, reddish, oily liquid, with a strong smell, like living raw meat. As for the bones left in the jar, from being black and putrid they had become white and clean and transparent like mother of pearl. I rubbed my legs with this liquid five times a day. And lo and behold, twenty-four hours later I found I could move my toes; another day and I could bend my legs and straighten them again. On the fifth day I stood on my feet, and with the help of a stick walked about the yard. In a word, in a week's time my legs had become fully as strong as they were before. I thanked God and mused upon the mysterious power which He has given His creatures. Dry, putrid bones, almost brought to dust, yet keeping such vital force, colour, smell, power of acting on living bodies, and as it were giving life to bodies that are half dead! It is a pledge of the future resurrection of the body. How I would like to point this out to that forester with whom I lived, in view of his doubts about the general resurrection!

Having in this way got better from my illness, I began to teach the boy. Instead of the usual copybook work, he wrote out the Prayer of Jesus. I made him copy it, showing him how to set out the words nicely. I found teaching the lad restful, for during the daytime he worked for the steward of an estate near by, and could only come to me while the steward slept, that is, from daybreak till the Liturgy.

He was a bright boy, and soon began to write fairly well. His employer saw him writing, and asked him who had taught him.

59

"A one-armed pilgrim who lives in our old bath-house," said the boy.

The steward, who was a Pole, was interested, and came to have a look at me. He found me reading *The Philokalia*, and started a talk by asking what I was reading. I showed him the book. "Ah," said he, "that's *The Philokalia*. I've seen the book before at our priest's [6] when I lived at Vilna. They tell me, however, that it contains odd sorts of schemes and tricks for prayer written down by the Greek monks. It's like those fanatics in India and Bokhara who sit down and blow themselves out trying to get a sort of tickling in their hearts, and in their stupidity take this bodily feeling for prayer, and look upon it as the gift of God. All that is necessary to fulfil one's duty to God is to pray simply, to stand and say the Our Father as Christ taught us. That puts you right for the whole day; but not to go on over and over again to the same tune. That, if I may say so, is enough to drive you mad. Besides, it's bad for your heart."

"Don't think in that way about this holy book, sir," I answered. "It was not written by simple Greek monks, but by great and very holy men of old time, men whom your Church honours also, such as Anthony the Great, Macarius the Great, Mark the spiritual Athlete, John Chrysostom and others. It was from them that the monks of India and Bokhara took over the ' heart method ' of interior prayer, only they quite spoilt and garbled it in doing so, as my *starets* explained to me. In *The Philokalia* all the teaching about the practice of

60

prayer in the heart is taken from the Word of God, from the Holy Bible, in which the same Jesus Christ who bade us say the Our Father taught also ceaseless prayer in the heart. For He said, ' *Thou shalt love the Lord thy God with all thy heart and with all thy mind,*' ' *Watch and pray,*' ' *Abide in Me and I in you.*' And the holy Fathers, calling to witness the holy King David's words in the Psalms, ' *O taste and see how gracious the Lord is,*' explain the passage thus : that the Christian man ought to use every possible means of seeking, and finding, delight in prayer, and ceaselessly to look for consolation in it, and not be content with simply saying ' Our Father ' once a day. Let me read to you how these saints blame those who do not strive to reach the gladness of the prayer of the heart. They write that such do wrong for three reasons, first because they show themselves against the Scriptures inspired by God, and secondly because they do not set before themselves a higher and more perfect state of soul to be reached. They are content with outward virtues only, and cannot hunger and thirst for the truth, and therefore miss the blessedness and joy in the Lord. Thirdly because, by letting their mind dwell upon themselves and their own outward virtues they often slip into temptation and pride, and so fall away.''

" It is sublime, what you are reading,'' said the steward, " but it's hardly for us ordinary lay folk, I think ! ''

" Well, I will read you something simpler, about how people of goodwill, even if living in the world, may learn how to pray without ceasing.''

I found the sermon on George the Youth, by Simeon

the New Theologian, and read it to him from *The Philokalia*.

This pleased him, and he said, " Give me that book to read at my leisure, and I will have a good look into it some time."

" I will let you have it for twenty-four hours with pleasure," I answered, " but not for longer, because I read it every day, and I just can't live without it."

" Well then, at least copy out for me what you have just read : I will pay you for your trouble."

" I don't want payment," said I. " I will write that out for you for love's sake and in the hope that God will give you a longing for prayer."

I at once and with pleasure made a copy of the sermon I had read. He read it to his wife, and both of them were pleased with it. And so it came about that at times they would send for me, and I would go, taking *The Philokalia* with me, and read to them while they sat drinking tea and listening. Once they asked me to stay to dinner. The steward's wife, who was a kindly old lady, was sitting with us at table eating some fried fish, when by some mischance she got a bone lodged in her throat. Nothing we could do gave her any relief, and nothing would move the bone. Her throat gave her so much pain that a couple of hours later she had to go and lie down. The doctor (who lived twenty miles away) was sent for, and as by this time it was evening, I went home, feeling very sorry for her.

That night, while I was sleeping lightly, I heard my *starets'* voice. I saw no figure, but I heard him say to me,

" The man you are living with cured you, why then do you not help the steward's wife ? God has bidden us feel for our neighbour."

" I would help her gladly," I answered, " but how ? I know no means whatever."

" Well, this is what you must do : from her very earliest years she has had a dislike of oil. She not only will not taste it, but cannot bear even the smell of it without being sick. So make her drink a spoonful of oil. It will make her vomit, the bone will come away, the oil will soothe the sore the bone has made in her throat, and she will be well again."

" And how am I to give it her, if she dislikes it so ? She will refuse to drink it."

" Get the steward to hold her head, and pour it suddently into her mouth, even if you have to use force."

I woke up, and went straight off and told the steward all this in detail. " What good can your oil do now ? " said he. " She is hoarse and delirious, and her neck is all swollen."

" Well, at any rate, let us try ; even if it doesn't help, oil is at least harmless as a medicine."

He poured some into a wineglass and somehow or other we got her to swallow it. She was violently sick at once, and soon vomited up the bone, and some blood with it. She began to feel easier, and fell into a deep sleep. In the morning I went to ask after her and found her sitting quietly taking her tea. Both she and her husband were full of wonder at the way she had been cured, and even greater than that was their surprise that her dislike of oil had been told me in a dream, for apart from themselves, not a soul knew of the fact. Just then the doctor also drove up, and the steward told him what had happened to his wife, and I in my turn told him how the peasant had cured my legs. The doctor listened to it all and then said, "Neither the one case nor the other is greatly to be wondered at, it is the same natural force which operated in both cases. Still, I shall make a note of it." And he took out a pencil and wrote in his notebook.

After this the report quickly spread through the whole neighbourhood that I was a prophet and a doctor and wizard. There began a ceaseless stream of visitors from all parts to bring their affairs and their troubles to my notice. They brought me presents and began to treat me with respect and to look after my comfort. I bore this for a week, and then, fearing I should fall into vain-glory and harmful distractions, I left the place in secret by night.

Thus once more I set out on my lonely way, feeling as light as if a great weight had been taken off my shoulders. The Prayer comforted me more and more, so that at times my heart bubbled over with boundless love for Jesus Christ, and from my delight in this streams of consolation seemed to flow through my whole being. The remembrance of Jesus Christ was so stamped upon my mind that as I dwelt upon the Gospel story I seemed to see its events before my very eyes. I was moved even to tears of joy, and sometimes felt such gladness in my heart that I am at a loss even how to tell of it.

The Way of a Pilgrim

It happened at times that for three days together I came upon no human dwelling, and in the uplifting of my spirit I felt as though I were alone on the earth, one wretched sinner before the merciful and man-loving God. This sense of being alone was a comfort to me, and it made me feel my delight in prayer much more than when I was mixing with a crowd of people.

At length I reached Irkutsk. When I had prayed before the relics of St. Innocent, I began to wonder where I should go now. I did not want to stay there for a long while, it was a town in which many people lived. I was walking thoughtfully along the street when I came upon a certain merchant belonging to the place. He stopped me saying, " Are you a pilgrim? Why not come home with me?" We went off together and he took me into his richly furnished house and asked me about myself. I told him all about my travels, and then he said, " You ought to go on a pilgrimage to Jerusalem, there are shrines there the like of which are not to be found anywhere else!"

" I should be only too glad to do so," I answered, " but I haven't the money. I can get along on dry land till I come to the sea, but I have no means of paying for a sea voyage, and it takes a good deal of money."

" How would you like me to find the money for you? I have already sent one of our townsfolk there, an old man, last year," said the merchant.

I fell at his feet, and he went on to say, " Listen, I will give you a letter to my son at Odessa. He lives there and has business connections with Constantinople. He will

65

be pleased to give you a passage on one of the vessels to Constantinople, and to tell his agents there to book a passage to Jerusalem for you on another boat, and pay for it. That is not so very expensive.''

I was overcome with joy when I heard this, and thanked my benefactor for his kindness. Even more did I thank God for showing me such fatherly love, and for His care for me, a wretched sinner, who did no good either to himself or to anyone else, and ate the bread of others in idleness. I stayed three days with this kindly merchant. As he had promised, he wrote me a letter to his son, so here I am now on my way to Odessa planning to go on till I reach Jerusalem. But I do not know whether the Lord will allow me to venerate His life-giving tomb.

3

JUST before leaving Irkutsk, I went to see my spiritual
father, with whom I had so often talked, and I said to
him, " Here I am actually off to Jerusalem. I have come
to say good-bye, and to thank you for your love for me
in Christ, unworthy pilgrim as I am."

" May God bless your journey," he replied. " But
how is it that you have never told me about yourself,
who you are nor where you come from ? I have heard
a great deal about your travels, and I should be interested
to know something about your birth and your life before
you became a pilgrim."

" Why, very gladly," I answered. " I will tell you all
about that also. It's not a very lengthy matter.

" I was born in a village in the government of Orel.
After the death of our parents, there were just the two of
us left, my brother and I, he was ten years old and I was
two. We were adopted by our grandfather, a worthy old
man and comfortably off. He kept an inn which stood
on the main road, and thanks to his sheer goodness of
heart, a lot of travellers put up there. My brother, who
was a madcap child, spent most of his time running
about in the village, but for my part I liked better to
stay near my grandfather. On Sundays and festivals we
used to go to church together, and at home my grandfather often used to read the Bible, this very Bible here,
which now belongs to me. When my brother grew up

he took to drink. Once when I was seven years old and we were both of us lying down on the stove, he pushed me so hard that I fell off and hurt my left arm, so that I have never been able to use it since, it is all withered up. My grandfather saw that I should never be fit to work on the land and taught me to read. As we had no spelling-book, he did so from this Bible. He pointed out the A's, and made me form words and learn to know the letters when I saw them. I scarcely know how myself, but, somehow, by saying things after him over and over again, I learned to read in the course of time. And later on, when my grandfather's sight grew weak he often made me read the Bible aloud to him, and he corrected me as he listened. There was a certain clerk who often came to our inn. He wrote a good hand and I liked watching him write. I copied his writing, and he began to teach me. He gave me paper and ink, he made me quill pens, and so I learned to write also. Grandfather was very pleased, and charged me thus, ' God has granted you the gift of learning ; it will make a man of you. Give thanks to God, and pray very often.'

" We used to attend all the services at church and we often had prayers at home. It was always my part to read the fifty-first psalm, and while I did so grandfather and grandmother made their prostrations or knelt. When I was seventeen I lost my grandmother. Then grandfather said to me, ' This house of ours no longer has a mistress, and that is not well. Your brother is a worthless fellow. I am going to look for a wife for you, you must get married.' I was against the idea, saying that I

68

was a cripple, but my grandfather would not give way. He found a worthy and sensible young girl about twenty years of age and I married her. A year later my grandfather fell very ill. Knowing that his death was near, he called for me, and bade me farewell, saying, ' I leave you my house and all I have. Obey your conscience, deceive no one, and above all pray to God ; everything comes from Him. Trust in Him only. Go to church regularly, read your Bible, and remember me and your grandmother in your prayers. Here is my money, that also I give you ; there is a thousand roubles. Take care of it. Do not waste it, but do not be miserly either ; give some of it to the poor and to God's church.' After this he died, and I buried him.

" My brother grew envious because the property had been left wholly to me. His anger against me grew, and the Enemy prompted him in this to such an extent that he even laid plans to kill me. In the end this is what he did one night while we were asleep and no guests were in the house. He broke into the room where the money was kept, stole the money from a chest and then set fire to the room. The fire had got a hold upon the whole building before we knew of it, and we only just escaped by jumping out of a window in our night clothes. The Bible was lying under our pillow, so we snatched it up and took it with us. As we watched our house burning we said to one another, ' Thank God, the Bible is saved, that at least is some consolation in our grief.' So everything we had was burnt, and my brother went off without a trace. Later on we heard that when he was in his cups he boasted of the fact that he had taken the money and burnt the house.

" We were left naked and ruined, absolutely beggars. We borrowed some money as best we could, built a little hut, and took up the life of landless peasants. My wife was clever with her hands. She knitted, spun and sewed. People gave her jobs, and day and night she worked and kept me. Owing to the uselessness of my arm I could not even make bark shoes. She would do her knitting and spinning, and I would sit beside her and read the Bible. She would listen, and sometimes begin to cry. When I asked, ' What are you crying about ? At least we are alive, thank God ! ' she would answer, ' It touches me so, that beautiful writing in the Bible.'

" Remembering what my grandfather had bidden us, we often fasted, every morning we said the Acathist of Our Lady, and at night we each made a thousand prostrations to avoid falling into temptation. Thus we lived quietly enough for two years. But this is what is so surprising—although we had no understanding of interior prayer offered in the heart and indeed had never heard of it, but prayed with the tongue only, and made our prostrations without thought like buffoons turning somersaults, yet in spite of all this the wish for prayer was there, and the long prayers we said without understanding did not seem tiring, indeed we liked them. Clearly it is true, as a certain teacher once told me, that a secret prayer lies hidden within the human heart. The man himself does not know it, yet working mysteriously within his soul, it urges him to prayer according to each man's knowledge and power.

"After two years of this sort of life that we were leading, my wife was taken suddenly ill with a high fever. She was given her Communion and on the ninth day of her illness she died. I was now left entirely alone in the world. There was no sort of work that I could do; still I had to live, and it went against my conscience to beg. Beside that, I felt such grief at the loss of my wife that I did not know what to do with myself. When I happened to go into our little hut and caught sight of her clothes or perhaps a scarf, I burst into tears and even fell down senseless. So feeling I could no longer bear my grief living at home, I sold the hut for twenty roubles, and such clothes as there were of my own and my wife's I gave away to the poor. Because of my crippled arm I was given a passport which set me free once for all from public duties, and taking my beloved Bible I set straight off, without caring or thinking where I was going.

"But after a while I began to think where I would go, and said to myself, 'First of all I will go to Kiev. I will venerate the shrines of those who were pleasing to God, and ask for their help in my trouble.' As soon as I had made up my mind to this, I began to feel better, and, a good deal comforted, I made my way to Kiev. Since that time, for the last thirteen years that is, I have gone on wandering from place to place, I have made the round of many churches and monasteries, but nowadays I am taking more and more to wandering over the steppes

71

and fields. I do not know whether God will vouchsafe to let me go to Jerusalem. If it be His will, when the time comes my sinful bones may be laid to rest there."

" And how old are you ? "

" Thirty-three."

" Well, dear brother, you have reached the age of Our Lord Jesus Christ ! "

4

' THE Russian proverb is true, which says that ' man proposes but God disposes,' " said I, as I came back again to my spiritual father. " I thought that by now I should certainly be on my way to Jerusalem. But see how differently things have fallen out. Something quite unlooked for has happened and kept me in the same place here for another three days. And I could not help coming to tell you about it and to ask your advice in making up my mind about the matter."

It happened like this. I had said good-bye to everybody, and with God's help started on my way. I had got as far as the outskirts of the town when I saw a man I knew standing at the door of the very last house. He was at one time a pilgrim like me, but I had not seen him for about three years. We greeted one another and he asked me where I was going.

" God willing," I answered, " I want to go to Jerusalem."

" Thank God! There is a nice fellow-traveller for you," he said.

" God be with you, and with him too," said I, " but surely you know that it is never my way to travel with other people. I always wander about alone."

" Yes, but listen. I feel sure that this one is just your

sort; you will suit each other down to the ground. Now, look here, the father of the master of this house, where I have been taken on as a servant, is going under a vow to Jerusalem, and you will easily get used to each other. He belongs to this town, he's a good old man, and what's more he is quite deaf. So much so that however much you shout, he can't hear a word. If you want to ask him anything you have to write it on a bit of paper, and then he answers. So you see he won't bore you on the road; he won't speak to you; even at home here he grows more and more silent. On the other hand you will be a great help to him on the way. His son is giving him a horse and cart, which he will take as far as Odessa and then sell there. The old man wants to go on foot, but the horse is going as well because he has a bit of luggage, and some things he is taking to the Lord's Tomb. And you can put your knapsack in with them too, of course. Now just think, how can we possibly send an old deaf man off with a horse, all by himself on such a long journey? They have searched and searched for somebody to take him, but they all want to be paid such a lot; besides, there's a risk in sending him with someone we don't know, for he has money and belongings with him. Say ' Yes,' brother, it will really be all right; make up your mind now for the glory of God and the love of your neighbour. I will vouch for you to his people, and they will be too pleased for words; they are kindly folk and very fond of me, I've been working for them for two years now."

All this talk had taken place at the door, and he now

took me into the house. The head of the household was there, and I saw clearly that they were quite a worthy and decent family. So I agreed to the plan. So now we have arranged to start with God's blessing, after hearing the Liturgy two days after Christmas. What unexpected things we meet with on life's journey! Yet all the while, God and His Holy Providence guide our actions and over-rule our plans, as it is written, " *It is God which worketh in you both to will and to do.*"

On hearing all this, my spiritual father said, " I rejoice with all my heart, dear brother, that God has so ordered it that I should see you again, so unexpectedly and so soon. And since you now have time, I want, in all love, to keep you a little longer, and you shall tell me more about the instructive experiences you have met with in the course of your long pilgrimages. I have already listened with great pleasure and interest to what you told me before."

" I am quite ready and happy to do that," I answered, and I began as follows :

A great many things have happened to me, some good and some bad. It would take a long while to tell of them all, and much I have already forgotten. For I have tried especially to remember only such matters as guided and urged my idle soul to prayer. All the rest I rarely remember ; or rather I have tried to forget the past, as St. Paul bids us when he says, " *Forgetting the things that are behind and stretching forward to the things that are before, I press on toward the goal of the prize of the high calling.*" My late *starets* of blessed memory also used to say that the forces which are against prayer in the heart attack us from two sides, from the left hand and from the right. That is to say, if the enemy cannot turn us from prayer by means of vain thoughts and sinful ideas, then he brings back into our minds good things we have been taught, and fills us with beautiful ideas, so that one way or another he may lure us away from prayer, which is a thing he cannot bear. It is called " a theft from the right hand side," and in it the soul, putting aside its converse with God, turns to the satisfaction of converse with self or with created things. He taught me, therefore, not to admit during times of prayer even the most lofty of spiritual thoughts. And if I saw that in the course of the day time had been spent more in improving thought and talk than in the actual hidden prayer of the heart, then I was to think of it as a loss of the sense of proportion, or a sign of spiritual greed. This is above all true, he said, in the case of beginners, for whom it is most needful that time given to prayer should be very much more than that taken up by other sides of the devout life.

Still one cannot forget everything. A matter may have printed itself so deeply in one's mind, that although it has not been actually thought of for a long time, yet it is remembered very clearly. A case in point is the few days' stay that God deemed me worthy to enjoy with a certain devout family in the following manner.

During my wanderings in the Tobolsk Government I happened to pass through a certain country town. My supply of dried bread had run very low, so I went to one of the houses to ask for some more. The householder said, "Thank God, you have come just at the right moment, my wife has only just taken the bread out of the oven, so there is a hot loaf for you. Remember me in your prayers." I thanked him and was putting the bread away in my knapsack, when his wife, who was looking on, said, "What a wretched state your knapsack is in, it is all worn out. I'll give you another instead." And she gave me a good strong one. I thanked them very heartily and went on. On leaving the town I went into a little shop to ask for a bit of salt, and the shopkeeper gave me a small bag quite full. I rejoiced in spirit and thanked God for leading me, unworthy as I was, to such kindly folk. "Now," thought I, "without having to worry about food I shall be filled and content for a whole week. Bless the Lord, O my soul!"

Three miles or so from this town the road I was following passed through a poor village, where I saw a little wooden church nicely decked out and painted on the outside. As I was going by it I felt a wish to honour God's house, and going into the porch I prayed for a while. On the grass at the side of the church there were playing two little children of five or six years of age. I took them to be the parish priest's children, for they were very nicely dressed. I finished my prayers and went on my way, but I had not gone a dozen paces from the church when I heard a shout behind me. "Dear little beggar! Dear little beggar! Stop!" The two little ones I had seen, a boy and a girl, were calling and running after me. I stopped and they ran up to me and took me by the hand. "Come along to mummy, she likes beggars."

"I'm not a beggar," I told them, "I'm just a passer-by."

"Why have you got a bag, then?"

"That is for the bread I eat on the way."

"All the same you must come. Mummy will give you some money for your journey."

"But where is your mummy?" I asked.

"Down there behind the church, behind that little wood."

They took me into a beautiful garden in the middle of which stood a large country house. We went inside, and how clean and smart it all was! The lady of the house comes hurrying to us. "Welcome, welcome! God has sent you to us; and how did you come? Sit down, sit down, dear." With her own hands she took off my knapsack and put it on a table, and made me sit in a very comfortably padded chair. "Wouldn't you like something to eat? Or a cup of tea? Isn't there anything you need?"

"I most humbly thank you," I answered, "but I have a whole bagful of food. It is true that I do take tea, but as a peasant I am not very used to it. I value your heart-felt and kindly welcome even more than the treat you offer me. I shall pray that God may bless you for show-ing such love for strangers in the spirit of the Gospels."

While I was speaking, a strong feeling came over me, urging me to withdraw within myself again. The Prayer was surging up in my heart, and I needed peace and silence to give free play to this quickening flame of prayer, as well as to hide from others the outward signs which went with it, such as tears and sighs and unusual movements of the face and lips. I therefore got up, saying, " Please excuse me, but I must leave now ; may the Lord Jesus Christ be with you and with your dear little children."

" Oh, no ! God forbid that you should go away. I won't allow it. My husband, who is a magistrate, will be coming back from town this evening, and how delighted he will be to see you ! He reverences every pilgrim as a messenger of God. If you go away he will be really grieved not to have seen you. Beside that, to-morrow is Sunday, and you will pray with us at the Liturgy, and at the dinner-table take your share with us in what God has sent. On holy days we always have up to thirty guests, and all of them our poor brothers in Jesus Christ. Come now, why have you told me nothing about yourself, where you come from and where you are going ? Talk to me, I like listening to the spiritual conversation of devout people. Children, children ! Take the pilgrim's knapsack into the oratory, he will spend the night there."

I was astonished as I listened to what she said, and I asked myself whether I was talking with a human being or with a ghost of some sort.

So I stayed, and waited for her husband. I gave her a short account of my travels, and said I was on my way to Irkutsk.

" Why, then, you will have to go through Tobolsk," said the lady, " and my own mother is a nun in a convent there, she is a *skhimnitsa* [7] now. We will give you a letter and she will be glad to see you. A great many people go to consult her on spiritual matters. And you will be able to take her a book by St. John of the Ladder which we have just ordered from Moscow at her request. How nicely it all fits in ! "

Soon it was dinner-time, and we sat down to table. Four other ladies came in and began the meal with us. When the first course was ended one of them rose, bowed to the Icon, [8] and then to us. Then she went and fetched the second course and sat down again. Then another of the ladies in the same way went and brought the third course. When I saw this, I said to my hostess, " May I venture to ask whether these ladies are relations of yours ? "

" Yes, they are indeed sisters to me ; this is my cook, and this the coachman's wife, that one has charge of the keys and the other is my maid. They are all married, I have no unmarried girls at all in my whole household."

The more I saw and heard of all this, the more surprised I was, and I thanked God for letting me see these devout people. I felt the prayer stirring strongly in my heart, so wishing to be alone as soon as I could and not hinder the prayer, I said to the lady as soon as we rose from the table, " No doubt you will rest for a while after dinner, and I am so used to walking that I will go for a stroll in the garden."

" No, I don't rest," she replied. " I will come into the garden with you, and you shall talk to me about something instructive. If you go alone, the children will give you no peace, directly they see you, they will not leave you for a minute, they are so fond of beggars, and brothers in Christ, and pilgrims."

There was nothing for me to do but to go with her. In order to avoid doing the talking myself, when we got into the garden I bowed down to the ground before her and said, " Do tell me, please, have you lived this devout life long, and how did you come to take it up ? "

" I will tell you the whole story if you like," was the answer. " You see my mother was a great-grand-daughter of St. Joasaph, whose relics rest at Byelgorod. We had a large town house, one wing of which was rented to a man who was a gentleman but not well off. After a while he died ; his wife was left pregnant and herself died in giving birth to a child. The infant was left an orphan and in poverty, and out of pity my mother adopted him. A year later I was born. We grew up together and did lessons together with the same tutors and governesses, and were as used to each other as a real brother and sister. Some while later my father died, and my mother gave up living in town and came with us to live on this estate of hers here. When we grew up, she gave me in marriage to her adopted son, settled this estate on us, and herself took the veil in a convent, where she had a cell built for her. She gave us a mother's blessing, and as her last will and testament she urged us to live as good Christians, to say our prayers fervently, and above all try to fulfil the greatest of God's command-ments, that is, the love of one's neighbour, to feed and help our poor brothers in Christ in simplicity and humility, to bring up our children in the fear of the

Lord, and to treat our serfs as our brothers. And that is how we have been living here by ourselves for the last ten years now, trying as best we could to carry out mother's last wishes. We have a guesthouse for beggars, and at the present moment there are living in it more than ten crippled and sick people. If you care to, we will go and see them to-morrow."

When she had ended her story, I asked her where the book by St. John of the Ladder was, which she wished to send to her mother. "Come indoors," she said, "and I will find it for you."

We had just sat down and begun to read it when her husband came in, and seeing me, gave me a warm welcome. We kissed each other as two brothers in Christ, and then he took me off to his own room, saying, "Come, dear brother, let us go into my study, and you shall bless my cell. I expect she (pointing to his wife) has been boring you. No sooner does she catch sight of a pilgrim of either sex, or of some sick person, than she is so delighted that she will not leave them day or night. She has been like that for years and years." We went into the study. What a lot of books there were, and beautiful icons, and the life-giving Cross with the Figure life-sized, and the Gospels lying near it! I said a prayer, and then, "You are in God's own Paradise here," I said. "Here is the Lord Jesus Christ Himself, and His most holy Mother, and the blessed Saints! And there," I went on, pointing to the books, "are the divine, living and everlasting words of their teaching. I expect you very often enjoy heavenly converse with them."

" Yes, I admit I am a great lover of reading," he answered.

" What sort of books are they you have here ? " I asked.

" I have a large number of religious books," was the answer. " Here you see are the Lives of the Saints for the whole year, and the works of St. John Chrysostom, and Basil the Great, and many other theologians and philosophers. I have a lot of volumes of sermons, too, by celebrated modern preachers. My library is worth about five hundred pounds."

" Haven't you anything on prayer ? "

" Yes, I am very fond of reading about prayer. Here is the very latest work on the subject, the work of a Petersburg priest." He took down a book on the Lord's Prayer and we began to read it with great enjoyment. A short while after the lady came in, bringing tea, followed by the children, who dragged in a large silver basket full of biscuits and cakes such as I had never tasted before in my life. My host took the book from me and handed it to his wife, saying, " Now we will get her to read ; she reads beautifully, and we will keep our strength up with the tea." So she began reading, and we listened. And as I listened I felt the action of the Prayer in my heart. The longer the reading went on the more the Prayer grew and made me glad. Suddenly I saw something flash quickly before my eyes, in the air as it were, like the figure of my departed *starets*. I started, and so as to hide the fact I said, " Excuse me, I must have dropped asleep for a moment."

Then I felt as though the soul of my *starets* made its way into my own, or gave light to it. I felt a sort of light in my mind, and a number of ideas about prayer came to me. I was just crossing myself and setting my will to put these ideas aside when the lady came to the end of the book and her husband asked me whether I had liked it, so that talking began again. " Very much," I answered, " the ' Our Father ' is the loftiest and most precious of all the written prayers we Christians have, for the Lord Jesus Christ Himself gave it to us. And the explanation of it which has just been read is very good, too, only it all deals for the most part with the active side of the Christian life, and in my reading of the holy Fathers I have come across a more speculative and mystical explanation of the prayer."

" In which of the Fathers did you read this ? "

" Well, in Maxim the Confessor, for example, and in Peter the Damascene, in *The Philokalia.*"

" Do you remember it ? Tell us about it, please."

" Certainly. The first words of the prayer, ' Our Father which art in Heaven ' are explained in your book as a call to brotherly love for one's neighbour, since we are all children of the one Father, and that is very true. But in the holy Fathers the explanation goes further and is more deeply spiritual. They say that when we use these words we should lift up our mind to heaven, to the Heavenly Father, and remember every moment that we are in the presence of God.

" The words ' Hallowed be Thy Name ' are explained in your book by the care we ought to have not to utter the Name of God except with reverence, nor to use it in a false oath, in a word that the Holy Name of God be spoken holily and not taken in vain. But the mystical writers see here a plain call to inward prayer of the heart; that is, that the most Holy Name of God may be stamped inwardly upon the heart and be hallowed by self-acting prayer and hallow all our feelings and all the powers of the soul. The words 'Thy Kingdom come' they explain thus—may inward peace and quiet and spiritual joy come to our hearts. In your book again, the words 'Give us this day our daily bread' are understood as asking for what we need for our bodily life, not for more than that, but for what is needed for ourselves and for the help of our neighbour. On the other hand, Maxim the Confessor understands by 'daily bread' the feeding of the soul with heavenly bread, *i.e.*, the Word of God, and the union of the soul with God, by dwelling upon Him in thought and the unceasing inward prayer of the heart."

"Ah, but the attainment of interior prayer is a very big business and almost impossible for lay folk," exclaimed my host; "we are lucky if we manage to say our ordinary prayers without slothfulness."

"Don't look at it in that way," said I. "If it were out of the question and quite too hard to do, God would not have bidden us all do it. His strength is made perfect in weakness. The holy Fathers, who speak from their own experience, offer us the means, and make the way to win the prayer of the heart easier. Of course, for hermits they give special and higher methods, but for those who live in the world their writings show ways which truly lead to interior prayer."

"I have never come across anything of that sort in my reading," he said.

"If you would care to hear it, may I read you a little from *The Philokalia*?" I asked, taking up my copy. I found Peter the Damascene's article, part 3, page 48, and read as follows: "'One must learn to call upon the Name of God, more even than breathing—at all times, in all places, in every kind of occupation. The Apostle says, "*Pray without ceasing*." That is, he teaches men to have the remembrance of God in all times and places and circumstances. If you are making something you must call to mind the Creator of all things, if you see the light, remember the Giver of it, if you see the heavens and the earth and the sea and all that is in them, wonder and praise the Maker of them. If you put on your clothes recall Whose gift they are and thank Him Who provides for your life. In short, let every action be a cause of your remembering and praising God, and lo! you will be praying without ceasing and therein your soul will always rejoice.' There, you see, this way of ceaseless prayer is simple and easy and within the reach of everybody so long as he has some amount of human feeling."

They were extraordinarily pleased with this. My host took me in his arms and thanked me again and again. Then he looked at my *Philokalia*, saying, "I must certainly buy myself a copy of this. I will get it at once from Petersburg; but for the moment and in memory of this occasion I will copy out the passage you have just read—you read it out to me." And then and there he wrote it out beautifully. Then he exclaimed, "Why, goodness me! Of course I have an icon of the Damascene!" (It was probably of St. John Damascene.) He picked up a frame, put what he had written behind the glass and hung it beneath the icon. "There," said he, "the living word of the Saint underneath his picture will often remind me to put his wholesome advice into practice."

After this we went to supper. As before, the whole household, men and women, sat down to table with us. How reverently silent and calm the meal was! And at the end of it we all, the children as well, spent a long while in prayer. I was asked to read the "Acathist to Jesus the Heart's Delight." Afterwards the servants went away to bed, and we three were left alone in the room. Then the lady brought me a white shirt and a pair of stockings. I bowed down at her feet, and said, "The stockings, little mother, I will not take. I have never worn them in my life, we are always so used to onoochi. [9]" She hurried off and brought back her old kaftan of thin yellow material, and cut it up into two onoochi, while her husband, saying, "And look, the poor fellow's footwear is almost worn out," brought me his new bashmaki,[10] large ones which he wore over his top boots. Then he told me to go into the next room, which was empty, and change my shirt. I did so, and when I came back to them again they sat me down on a chair to put my new footwear on, he wrapping my feet and legs in the onoochi and she putting on the *bashmaki*. At first I would not let them, but they bade me sit down, saying " Sit down and be quiet, Christ washed His disciples' feet." There was nothing to do but obey, and I began to weep, and so did they. After this the lady went to bed with the children, and her husband and I went to a summerhouse in the garden.

For a long while we did not go to sleep, but lay talking. He began in this way, " Now in God's name and on your conscience tell me the real truth. Who are you ? You must be of good birth, and are only assuming a disguise of simplicity. You read and write well, you speak correctly, and are able to discuss things, and these things do not go with a peasant upbringing."

" I spoke the real truth with a sincere heart both to you and to your wife when I told you about my birth, and I never had a thought of lying or of deceiving you. Why should I ? As for the things I say, they are not my own, but what I have heard from my departed *starets*, who was full of divine wisdom ; or what I have gathered from a careful reading of the holy Fathers. But my ignorance has gained more light from interior prayer than from anything else, and that I have not reached by myself, it has been granted me by the mercy of God and the teaching of my *starets*. And that can be done by anyone. It costs nothing but the effort to sink down in silence into the depths of one's heart and call more and more upon the radiant Name of Jesus. Everyone who does that feels at once the inward light, everything becomes understandable to him, he even catches sight in

88

this light of some of the mysteries of the Kingdom of God. And what depth and light there is in the mystery of a man coming to know that he has this power to plumb the depths of his own being, to see himself from within, to find delight in self-knowledge, to take pity on himself and shed tears of gladness over his fall and his spoiled will! To show good sense in dealing with things and to talk with people is no hard matter, and lies within anyone's power, for the mind and the heart were there before learning and human wisdom. If the mind is there, you can set it to work either upon science or upon experience, but if the mind is lacking then no teaching, however wise, and no training will be any good. The trouble is that we live far from ourselves and have but little wish to get any nearer to ourselves. Indeed we are running away all the time to avoid coming face to face with our real selves, and we barter the truth for trifles. We think, 'I would very gladly take an interest in spiritual things, and in prayer, but I have no time, the fuss and cares of life give no chance for such a thing.' Yet which is really important and necessary, salvation and the eternal life of the soul, or the fleeting life of the body on which we spend so much labour? It is that that I spoke of, and that leads to either sense or stupidity in people."

"Forgive me, dear brother, I asked not just out of mere curiosity, but from friendliness and Christian sympathy, and even more because about two years ago I came across a case which gave rise to the question I put to you. It was like this: There came to our house a certain beggar with a discharged soldier's passport. He was old and feeble, and so poor that he was almost naked and barefoot. He spoke little, and in such a simple way that you would take him for a peasant of the steppes. We took him into the guesthouse, but some five days later he fell seriously ill, and so we moved him to this very summerhouse, where we kept him quiet, and my wife and I looked after him and nursed him. But after a while it was plain that he was nearing his end. We prepared him for it, and sent for our priest for his Confession, Communion and Anointing. The day before he died, he got up and asked me for a sheet of paper and a pen, and begged me to shut the door and to let no one in while he wrote his will, which he desired me to send after his death to his son at an address in Petersburg. I was astounded when I saw him write, for not only did he write a beautiful and absolutely cultured hand, but the composition also was excellent, thoroughly correct and showing great delicacy of touch. In fact, I'll read you that will of his to-morrow. I have a copy of it. All this set me wondering, and aroused my curiosity enough to ask him about his origin and his life.

"After making me solemnly vow not to reveal it to anyone until after his death, he told me, for the glory of God, the story of his life. 'I was Prince X——,' he began. 'I was very wealthy and led a most luxurious and dissipated life. After the death of my wife, my son and I lived together, he being happily settled in military service; he was a captain in the Guards. One day when I was getting ready to go to a ball at an important person's house, I was very angry with my valet. Unable to control my temper, I struck him a severe blow on the head and ordered him to be sent away to his village. This happened in the evening, and next morning the valet died from the effects of the blow. This did not affect me very seriously. I regretted my rashness, but soon forgot the whole thing. Six weeks later, though, I began seeing the dead valet; in my dreams to begin with; every night he disturbed me and reproached me, incessantly repeating, " Conscienceless man! You are my murderer! " As time went on I began seeing him when I was awake also, wide awake. His appearances grew more and more frequent with the lapse of time, till the agitation he caused me became almost constant. And in the end he did not appear alone, but I saw at the same time other dead men whom I had treated very badly, and women whom I had seduced. They all reproached me ceaselessly and gave me no peace, to such an extent that I could neither sleep nor eat nor do anything else. My strength grew utterly exhausted, and my skin stuck to my bones. All the efforts of skilled physicians were of no avail at all. I went abroad for a cure, but after trying it for six months, I was not benefited in the slightest degree, and those torturing apparitions grew steadily worse and worse. I was brought home again more dead than alive. I went through the horrors and tortures of Hell in fullest measure. I had proof then that Hell exists, and I knew what it meant!

" ' While I was in this wretched condition I recognised

my own wrong-doing. I repented and made my confession. I gave all my serfs their freedom, and took a vow to afflict myself for the rest of my days with as toilsome a life as possible, and to disguise myself as a beggar. I wanted, because of all my sins, to become the humblest servant of people of the very lowest station in life. No sooner had I resolutely come to this decision than those disturbing visions of mine ceased. I felt such comfort and happiness from having made my peace with God that I cannot adequately describe it. But just as I had been through Hell before, so now I experienced Paradise, and learned what that meant also, and how the Kingdom of God is revealed in our hearts. I soon got perfectly well again and carried out my intention, leaving my native land secretly, furnished with a discharged soldier's passport. And now for the last fifteen years I have been wandering about the whole of Siberia. Sometimes I hire myself out to the peasants for such work as I can do. Sometimes I find sustenance by begging in the Name of Christ. Ah, what blessedness and what happiness and what peace of mind I enjoy in the midst of all these privations! It can be felt to the full only by one who by the mercy of the Great Intercessor has been brought out of Hell into Paradise.'

" When he came to the end of his story he handed me the will to forward to his son, and on the following day he died. And I have a copy of that will in a wallet lying on my Bible. If you would like to read it I will get it for you now. . . . Here you are."

I unfolded it and read thus: " In the Name of God

the glorious Trinity, the Father, the Son and the Holy Ghost.

" My dearest Son,
" It is fifteen years now since you saw your father. But though you have had no news of him, he has from time to time found means to hear of you, and cherished a father's love for you. That love impels him to send you these few lines from his deathbed. May they be a life-long lesson to you!
" You know how I suffered for my careless and thought-less life; but you do not know how I have been blessed in my unknown pilgrimage and filled with joy in the fruits of repentance.
" I die at peace in the house of one who has been good to me, and to you also; for kindnesses showered upon the father must touch the feeling heart of a grateful son. Render to him my gratitude in any way you can.
" In bestowing on you my paternal blessing, I adjure you to remember God and to guard your conscience. Be prudent, kindly and considerate; treat your inferiors as benevolently and amiably as you can; do not despise beggars and pilgrims, remembering that only in beggary and pilgrimage did your dying father find rest and peace for his tormented soul. I invoke God's blessing upon you, and calmly close my eyes in the hope of life eternal, through the mercy of the Great Intercessor for men, Our Lord Jesus Christ.

" Your Father X——."

Thus my host and I lay and chatted together; and in my turn I put a question to him. "I suppose you are not without worries and bothers, with this guesthouse of yours? Of course there are quite a lot of our pilgrim brotherhood who take to the life because they have nothing to do, or from sheer laziness, and sometimes they do a little thieving on the road; I have seen it myself."

"There have not been many cases of that sort," was the answer. "We have for the most part always come across genuine pilgrims. And if we do get the other sort, we welcome them all the more kindly and try the harder to get them to stay with us. Through living with our good beggars and brothers in Christ they often become reformed characters and leave the guesthouse humble and kindly folk. Why, there was a case of that sort not so long ago. He was a man belonging to the lower middle class of our town here, and he went so thoroughly to the bad that it came to the point of everybody driving him away from their doors with a stick and refusing to give him even a crust of bread. He was a drunken, quarrelsome bully, and what is more he stole. That was the sort of person he was when one day he came to us, very hungry, and asked for some bread and wine, for the latter of which he was extraordinarily eager. We gave him a friendly reception and said, 'Stay with us and we will give you as much wine as you like, but only on this condition, that when you have been drinking, you go straight away and lie down and go to sleep. If you get in the slightest degree unruly or troublesome, not

94

only shall we turn you out and never take you back again, but I shall report the matter to the police and have you sent off to a penal settlement as a suspected vagabond.' He agreed to this and stopped with us. For a week or more he certainly did drink a great deal, to his heart's content. But because of his promise and because of his attachment to the wine, which he was afraid of being deprived of, he always lay down to sleep afterwards, or took himself off to the kitchen garden and lay down there quietly enough. When he was sober again the brothers of the guesthouse talked persuasively to him and gave him good advice about learning to control himself, if only little by little to begin with. So he gradually began to drink less, and in the end, some three months later, he became quite a temperate person. He has taken a situation somewhere now, and no longer leads a futile life of dependence on other people's charity. The day before yesterday he came here to thank me."

What wisdom! I thought, made perfect by the guidance of love! and aloud I said, " Blessed be God, who has so shown His grace in the household under your care." After this talk we slept for an hour or an hour and a half till we heard the bells for Mattins. We got ready and went over to the church. On going in we at once saw the lady of the house, who had been there some time already with her children. We were all present at Mattins, and the Divine Liturgy went straight on afterwards. The head of the house with his little boy and I took our places within the altar,[11] while his wife and the little girl stood near the altar window, where they could

95

see the Elevation of the Holy Gifts. How earnestly they prayed as they knelt and shed tears of joy! And I wept to the full myself as I looked at the light on their faces. After the service was over, the gentlefolk, the priest, the servants and the beggars all went off together to the dining-room. There were some forty or so beggars, and cripples and sick folk and children. They all sat down at one and the same table, and how peaceful and silent it all was! I plucked up my courage, and said quietly to my host, " They read the lives of the saints during meals in monasteries. You might do the same. You've got the whole series of books."

" Let us adopt the plan here, Mary," said he, turning to his wife, " it will be most edifying. I will begin, and read at the first dinner-time, then you at the next, then the *batyushka*,[12] and after that the rest of the brothers who know how to read, in turn."

The priest began to talk and eat at the same time. " I like listening, but as for reading—well, with all respect I should like to be let off. You have no idea what a whirl I live in when I get home, worries and jobs of all sorts, first one thing has to be done and then another, what with a host of children and animals into the bargain —my whole day is filled up with things to do. There's no time for reading or study. I've long ago forgotten even what I learned at the seminary." I shuddered as I heard this, but our hostess, who was sitting near me, took my hand and said, " *Batyushka* talks like that because he is so humble, he always makes little of himself, but he is really a man of most kindly and saintly life. He has

96

been a widower for the last twenty years, and is bringing up a whole family of grandchildren. For all that he holds services very frequently." At these words there came into my mind the following saying of Nicetas Stethatus in *The Philokalia*. "The nature of things is judged by the inward disposition of the soul," that is, a man gets his ideas about his neighbours from what he himself is. And he goes on to say, "He who has attained to true prayer and love has no sense of the differences between things : he does not distinguish the righteous man from the sinner, but loves them all equally and judges no man, as God causes His sun to shine and His rain to fall on the just and the unjust."

We fell silent again. Opposite me sat one of the beggars from the guesthouse who was quite blind. The master of the house was looking after him. He cut up his fish for him, gave him his spoon and poured out his soup.

I watched carefully and saw that this beggar always had his mouth open and that his tongue was moving all the time, as though it were trembling. Surely, thought I, he must be one of those who pray. And I went on watching. Right at the end of dinner an old woman was taken ill. It was a sharp attack, and she began to groan. Our host and his wife took her into their bed-room and laid her on their bed, where the lady stayed to look after her. Her husband meanwhile ordered his carriage and went off at a gallop to the town for a doctor. The priest went to fetch the Reserved Sacrament, and we all went our ways.

I felt as it were hungry for prayer, an urgent need to pour out my soul in prayer, and I had not been in quiet nor alone for forty-eight hours. I felt as though there were in my heart a sort of flood struggling to burst out and flow through all my limbs. To hold it back caused me severe, even if comforting, pain in the heart, a pain which needed to be calmed and satisfied in the silence of prayer. And now I saw why those who really practise interior self-acting prayer have fled from the company of men and hidden themselves in unknown places. I saw further why the venerable Isikhi called even the most spiritual and helpful talk mere idle chatter if there were too much of it, just as Ephrem the Syrian says, " Good speech is silver, but silence is pure gold."

As I thought all this over, I made my way to the guesthouse, where everyone was resting after dinner. I went up into the attic, where I quietly rested and prayed.

When the beggars were about again I found the blind man and took him off to the kitchen garden, where we sat down alone and began to talk. " Tell me, please," said I, " do you for the sake of your soul say the Prayer of Jesus ? "

" I have said it without stopping for a long while."

" But what sort of feeling do you get from it ? "

" Only this, that day or night I cannot live without the Prayer."

" How did God show it you ? Tell me about it, tell me everything, dear brother."

" Well, it was like this. I belong to this district and

used to earn my living by doing tailoring jobs. I travelled about different provinces going from village to village, and made clothes for the peasants. I happened to stay a fairly long time in one village in the house of a peasant for whose family I was making clothing. One day, a holy day it was, I saw three books lying near the icons, and I asked who it was in the household that could read. 'No one,' they answered; 'those books were left us by an uncle; he knew how to read and write.' I picked up one of the books, opened it at random, and read, as I remember to this very hour, the following words: 'Ceaseless prayer is to call upon the Name of God always, whether a man is conversing, or sitting down, or walking, or making something, or eating, whatever he may be doing, in all places and at all times, he ought to call upon God's name.' Reading that started me thinking how simple that would be for me. I began to say the prayer in a whisper while I was sewing, and I liked it. People living in the same house with me noticed it, and began to make fun of me. 'Are you a wizard or what?' they asked, 'going on whispering all the time?' or 'What are you muttering charms about?' So to hide what I was doing I gave up moving my lips and went on saying the Prayer with my tongue only. In the end I got so used to the Prayer that my tongue went on saying it by itself day and night, and I liked it. I went about like that for a long while, and then all of a sudden I became quite blind. Almost everyone in our family gets 'dark water' [13] in the eyes. So, because I was so poor, our people got me into the almshouse at

Tobolsk, which is the capital of our province. I am on my way there now, only the gentry have kept me here because they want to give me a cart as far as Tobolsk."

"What was the name of the book you read? Wasn't it called *The Philokalia*?"

"Honestly, I don't know. I didn't even look at the title page."

I fetched my *Philokalia* and looked out in part 4 those very words of the Patriarch Callistus which he had said by heart, and I read them to him.

"Why, those are the very same words!" cried the blind man. "How splendid! Go on reading, brother."

When I got to the lines, "One ought to pray with the heart," he began to ply me with questions. "What does that mean? How is that done?"

I told him that full teaching on praying with the heart was given in this same book, *The Philokalia*. He begged me eagerly to read the whole thing to him.

"This is what we will do," said I. "When are you starting for Tobolsk?"

"Straight away," he answered.

"Very well then, I am also going to take the road again to-morrow. We will go together and I will read it all to you, all about praying with the heart, and I will show you how to find where your heart is, and to enter it."

"And what about the cart?" he asked.

"What does the cart matter! We know how far it is to Tobolsk, a mere hundred miles. We will take it easy, and think how nice it will be going along, just we two together alone, talking and reading about the Prayer as we go." And so it was agreed.

In the evening our host came himself to call us all to supper, and after the meal we told him that the blind man and I were taking the road together, and that we did not need a cart, so as to be able to read *The Philokalia* more easily. Hearing this he said, "I also liked *The Philokalia* very much, and I have already written a letter and got the money ready to send to Petersburg when I go into court to-morrow, so as to get a copy sent me by return of post."

So we set off on our way next morning, after thanking them very warmly for their great love and kindness. Both of them came with us for more than half a mile from their house. And so we bade each other good-bye.

We went on, the blind man and I, by easy stages, doing from six to ten miles a day. All the rest of the time we spent sitting down in lonely places and reading *The Philokalia*. I read him the whole part about praying with the heart, in the order which my departed *starets* had shown me, *i.e.*, beginning with the writings of Nicephorus the Monk, Gregory of Sinai, and so on. How eagerly and closely he listened to it all, and what happiness and joy it brought him! Then he began to put such questions to me about prayer as my mind was not equal to finding answers to. When we had read what we needed from *The Philokalia* he eagerly begged me actually to show him the way the mind finds the heart, how to bring the Divine Name of Jesus Christ into it, and how to find the joy of praying inwardly with the heart. And I told him all about it thus, " Now you, as a blind man, can see nothing. Yet as a matter of fact you can imagine with your mind and picture to yourself what you have seen in time past, such as a man or some object or other, or one of your own limbs. For instance, can you not picture your hand or your foot as clearly as if you were looking at it, can you not turn your eyes to it and fix them upon it, blind as they are ? "

" Yes, I can," he answered.

" Then picture to yourself your heart in just the same way, turn your eyes to it just as though you were looking at it through your breast, and picture it as clearly as you can. And with your ears listen closely to its beating, beat by beat. When you have got into the way of doing this, begin to fit the words of the Prayer to the beats of the heart one after the other, looking at it all the time. Thus, with the first beat, say or think ' Lord,' with the second, ' Jesus,' with the third, ' Christ,' with the fourth, ' have mercy,' and with the fifth ' on me.' And do it over and over again. This will come easily to you, for you already know the groundwork and the first part of praying with the heart. Afterwards, when you have grown used to what I have just told you about, you must begin bringing the whole Prayer of Jesus into and out of your heart in time with your breathing, as the Fathers taught. Thus, as you draw your breath in, say, or imagine yourself saying, ' Lord Jesus Christ,' and as you breathe again, ' have mercy on me.' Do this as often and as much as you can, and in a short space of time you will feel a slight and not unpleasant pain in your heart, followed by a warmth. Thus by God's help you will get the joy of self-acting inward prayer of the heart. But then, whatever you do, be on your guard against imagination and any sort of visions. Don't accept any of them whatever, for the holy Fathers lay down most strongly that inward prayer should be kept free from visions, lest one fall into temptation."

The blind man listened closely to all this, and began eagerly to do with his heart what I had shown him, and he spent a long while at it, especially during the night-time at our halting places. In about five days' time he began to feel the warmth very much, as well as a happiness beyond words in his heart, and a great wish to devote himself unceasingly to this Prayer which stirred up in him a love of Jesus Christ.

From time to time he saw a light, though he could make out no objects in it. And sometimes, when he made the entrance into his heart, it seemed to him as though a flame, as of a lighted candle, blazed up strongly and happily in his heart, and rushing outwards through his throat flooded him with light; and in the light of this flame he could see even far-off things; and this did indeed happen once. We were walking through a forest, and he was silent, wholly given up to the Prayer. Suddenly he said to me, "What a pity! The church is already on fire; there, the belfry has fallen."

"Stop this vain dreaming," I answered, "it is a temptation to you. You must put all such fancies aside at once. How can you possibly see what is happening in the town? We are still seven or eight miles away from it."

He obeyed me and went on with his Prayer in silence. Towards evening we came to the town, and there as a matter of fact I saw several burnt houses and a fallen belfry, which had been built with ties of timber, and people crowding around and wondering how it was that the belfry had crushed no one in its fall. As I worked it out, the misfortune had happened at the very same time as the blind man spoke to me about it. And he began to talk to me on the matter. "You told me," said he, "that this vision of mine was vain, but here you see things really are as I saw them. How can I fail to thank and to love the Lord Jesus Christ, Who shows His grace even to sinners and the blind and the foolish! And I thank you also for teaching me the work of the heart."

"Love Jesus Christ," said I, "and thank Him all you will. But beware of taking your visions for direct revelations of grace. For these things may often happen quite naturally in the order of things. The human soul is not bound by place and matter. It can see even in the darkness, and what happens a long way off, as well as things near at hand. Only we do not give force and scope to this spiritual power. We crush it beneath the yoke of our gross bodies or get it mixed up with our haphazard thoughts and ideas. But when we concentrate within ourselves, when we draw away from everything around us and become more subtle and refined in mind, then the soul comes into its own and works to its fullest power. So what happened was natural enough. I have heard my departed *starets* say that there are people (even such as are not given to prayer, but who have this sort of power, or gain it during sickness) who see light even in the darkest of rooms, as though it streamed from every article in it, and see things by it ; who see their doubles and enter into the thoughts of other people. But what does come direct from the grace of God in the case of the prayer of the heart, is so full of sweetness and delight that no tongue can tell of it, nor can it be likened to anything material, it is beyond compare. Every feeling is base compared with the sweet knowledge of grace in the heart."

My blind friend listened eagerly to this, and became still more humble. The prayer grew more and more in his heart, and delighted him beyond words. I rejoiced at this with all my soul, and thanked God from my heart that He had let me see so blessed a servant of His. We got to Tobolsk at last. I took him to the almshouse, and leaving him there with a loving farewell, I went on my own way.

I went along without hurrying for about a month with a deep sense of the way in which good lives teach us and spur us on to copy them. I read *The Philokalia* a great deal, and there made sure of everything I had told the blind man of prayer. His example kindled in me zeal and thankfulness and love for God. The Prayer of my heart gave me such consolation that I felt there was no happier person on earth than I, and I doubted if there could be greater and fuller happiness in the kingdom of

Heaven. Not only did I feel this in my own soul, but the whole outside world also seemed to me full of charm and delight. Everything drew me to love and thank God; people, trees, plants, animals. I saw them all as my kinsfolk, I found on all of them the magic of the Name of Jesus. Sometimes I felt as light as though I had no body and was floating happily through the air instead of walking. Sometimes when I withdrew into myself I saw clearly all my internal organs, and was filled with wonder at the wisdom with which the human body is made. Sometimes I felt as joyful as if I had been made Tsar. And at all such times of happiness, I wished that God would let death come to me quickly, and let me pour out my heart in thankfulness at His feet in the world of spirits.

It would seem that somehow I took too great a joy in these feelings, or perhaps it was just allowed by God's will, but for some time I felt a sort of quaking and fear in my heart. Was there, I wondered, some new misfortune or trouble coming upon me like what happened after I met the girl again to whom I taught the Prayer of Jesus in the chapel? A cloud of such thoughts came down upon me, and I remembered the words of the venerable John Karpathisky, who says that "The master will often submit to humiliation and endure disaster and temptation for the sake of those who have profited by him spiritually." I fought against the gloomy thoughts, and prayed with more earnestness than ever. The Prayer quite put them to flight, and taking heart again I said, "God's will be done, I am ready to suffer whatever

Jesus Christ sends me for my wickedness and pride. And those to whom I had lately shown the secret of entry into the heart and interior prayer had even before· their meeting with me been made ready by the direct and secret teaching of God."

Calmed by these thoughts, I went on my way again filled with consolation, having the Prayer with me and happier even than I had been before. It rained for a couple of days, and the road was so muddy that I could hardly drag my feet out of the mire. I was walking across the steppe, and in ten miles or so I did not find a single dwelling. At last towards nightfall I came upon one house standing by itself right on the road. Glad I was to see it, and I thought I would ask for a rest and a night's lodging here and see what God sent for the morrow; perhaps the weather would get better. As I drew near I saw a tipsy old man in a soldier's cloak sitting on the *zavalina*. I greeted him, saying, " Could I perhaps ask someone to give me a night's lodging here ? "

" Who else could give it you but me ? " he shouted. " I'm master here. This is a post-house and I am in charge of it."

" Then will you allow me, sir, to spend the night at your house ? "

" Have you got a passport ? Give some legal account of yourself."

I handed him my passport, and, holding it in his hands, he again asked, " Where is your passport ? "

" You have it in your hands," I answered.

" Well, come into the house," said he.

He put his spectacles on, read the passport through, and said, " All right, that's all in order. Stay the night. I'm a good fellow really. Have a drink."

" I don't drink," I answered, " and never have."

" Well, please yourself, I don't care. At any rate have supper with us."

They sat down to table, he and the cook, a young woman who also had been drinking rather freely, and asked me to sit down with them. They quarrelled all through supper, hurling reproaches at each other, and in the end came to blows. The man went off into the passage and to his bed in a lumber-room, while the cook began to tidy up and wash up the cups and spoons, all the while going on with the abuse of her master. I took a seat, thinking it would be some time before she quieted down. So I asked her where I could sleep, for I was very tired from my journey. " I will make you up a bed," she answered. And she placed another bench against the one under the front window, spread a felt blanket over them, and gave me a pillow. I lay down and shut my eyes as though asleep. For a long while yet the cook bustled about, but at last she tidied up, put out the fire, and was coming over towards me. Suddenly the whole window, which was in a corner at the front of the house, frame, glass and splinters of wood, flew into shivers which came showering down with a frightful crash. The whole house shook, and from outside the window came a sickening groan, and shouts and the noise of struggling. The woman sprang back in terror into the middle of the room and fell in a heap on the floor. I jumped up with my wits all astray, thinking the earth had opened under my feet. And the next thing is I see two drivers carrying a man into the house so covered with blood that you could not even see his face. And this added still more to my horror. He was a king's messenger who had galloped here to change horses. His driver had not taken the turn into the gateway properly, the carriage pole stove in the window, and as there was a ditch in front of the house, the carriage overturned and the king's messenger was thrown out, cutting his head badly on a sharp post.

He asked for some water and wine to bathe his wound. Then he drank a glass, and cried, " Horses ! "

I went up to him and said, " Surely, sir, you won't travel any further with a wound like that ? "

" A king's messenger has no time to be ill," he answered, and galloped off.

The drivers dragged the senseless woman into a corner near the stove, and covered her with a rug, saying, " She was badly scared. She'll come round all right." The master of the house had another glass, and went back to bed, and I was left alone. Very soon the woman got up again and began walking across the room from corner to corner in a witless sort of way, and in the end she went out of the house. I felt as though the shock had taken all the strength out of me, and after saying my prayers I dropped asleep for a while before dawn.

In the morning I took leave of the old man and set off

again, and as I walked I sent up my Prayer with faith and trust and thanks to the Father of all blessing and consolation Who had saved me when I was in such great danger.

Some six years after this happened I was passing a convent and went into the church to pray. The kindly abbess welcomed me in her room after the Liturgy, and had tea served. Suddenly some unexpected guests came to see her, and she went to them, leaving me with some of the nuns who waited on her in her cell. One of them, who was pouring out tea, and was clearly a humble soul, made me curious enough to ask whether she had been in the convent long.

" Five years," she answered. " I was out of my mind when they brought me here, and it was here that God had mercy on me. The mother abbess kept me to wait on her in her cell and led me to take the veil."

" How came you to go out of your mind ? " I asked.

" It was fright," said she. " I used to work at a post-house and late one night some horses stove in a window. I was so terrified that it drove me out of my mind. For a whole year my relations took me from one shrine to another, but it was only here that I got cured." When I heard this I rejoiced in spirit, and praised God, Who so wisely orders all things for the best.

" I had a great many other experiences," I said, speaking to my spiritual father, " but I should want three whole days and nights to tell you everything as it happened. Still there is one other thing I will tell you about."

One clear summer's day I noticed a cemetery near the road, and what they call a *pogost*, *i.e.*, a church with some houses for those who minister in it. The bells were ringing for the Liturgy, and I made my way towards it. People who lived round about were going the same way, and some of them, before they got as far as the church, were sitting on the grass. Seeing me hurrying along, they said to me, " Don't hurry, you'll have plenty of time for standing about when the service begins. Services take a long while here : our priest is in bad health and goes very slowly."

The service did, in fact, last a very long while. The priest was a young man, but very thin and pale. He celebrated very slowly indeed, but with great devotion, and at the end of the Liturgy he preached with much feeling a beautiful and simple sermon on how to grow in love for God. The priest asked me into his house and to stay to dinner.

During the meal I said," How reverently and slowly you celebrate, Father ! "

" Yes," he answered, " but my parishioners do not like it, and they grumble. Still, there's nothing to be done about it. I like to meditate on each prayer and rejoice in it before I say it aloud. Without that interior appreciation and feeling every word uttered is useless both to myself and to others. Everything centres in the interior life, and in attentive prayer ! Yet how few concern themselves with the interior life," he went on.

" It is because they feel no desire to cherish the spiritual inward light."

" And how is one to reach that ? " I asked. " It would seem to be very difficult."

" Not at all," was the reply. " To attain spiritual enlightenment and become a man of recollected interior life, you should take some one text or other of Holy Scripture and for as long a period as possible concentrate on that alone all your power of attention and meditation ; then the light of understanding will be revealed to you. You must proceed in the same way about prayer. If you want it to be pure, right and enjoyable, you must choose some short prayer, consisting of few but forcible words, and repeat it frequently and for a long while. Then you will find delight in prayer."

This teaching of the priest pleased me very much. How practical and simple it was, and yet at the same time how deep and how wise. I gave thanks to God, in my thoughts, for showing me such a true pastor of his church.

When the meal was over, he said to me, " You have a sleep after dinner while I read the Bible and prepare my sermon for to-morrow." So I went into the kitchen. There was no one there except a very old woman sitting crouched in a corner coughing. I sat down under a small window, took *The Philokalia* out of my knapsack, and began to read quietly to myself. After a while I heard the old woman who was sitting in the corner ceaselessly whispering the Prayer of Jesus. It gave me great joy to hear the Lord's most holy Name spoken so often, and I said to her, " What a good thing it is, mother, that you are always saying the Prayer. It is a most Christian and most wholesome action."

" Yes," she replied. " The ' Lord have mercy ' is the only thing I have to lean on in my old age."

" Have you made a habit of this prayer for long ? "

" Since I was quite young ; yes, and I couldn't live without it, for the Jesus Prayer saved me from ruin and death."

" How ? Please tell me about it, for the glory of God and in praise of the blessed power of the Prayer of Jesus."

I put *The Philokalia* away in my knapsack and took a seat nearer to her, and she began her story.

" I used to be a young and pretty girl. My parents gave me in marriage, and the very day before the wedding, my bridegroom came to see us. Suddenly, before he had taken a dozen steps, he dropped down and died, without a single gasp. This frightened me so that I utterly refused to marry at all. I made up my mind to live unmarried, to go on pilgrimage to the shrines, and pray at them. However, I was afraid to travel all by myself, young as I was, I feared evil people might molest me. But an old woman-pilgrim whom I knew taught me wherever my road took me always to say the Jesus Prayer without stopping, and told me for certain that if I did no misfortune of any sort could happen to me on my way. I proved the truth of this, for I walked even to far-off shrines and never came to any harm. My parents gave me the money for my journeys. As I grew old I lost my health, and now the priest here out of the kindness of his heart gives me board and lodging."

I was overjoyed to hear this, and knew not how to thank God for this day, in which I had been taught so much by examples of spiritual life. Then, asking the kindly and devout priest for his blessing, I set off again on my way rejoicing.

Then again, not so long ago, as I was making my way here through the Kazan Government, I had a chance of learning how the power of prayer in the Name of Jesus Christ is shown clearly and strongly even in those who use it without a will to do so, and how saying the Prayer often and for a long time is a sure and rapid way to gaining its blessed fruits. It happened that I was to pass the night at a Tartar village. On reaching it I saw a Russian carriage and coachman outside the window of one of the huts. The horses were being fed near by. I was glad to see all this, and made up my mind to ask for a night's lodging at the same place, thinking that I should at least spend the night with Christians.[14] When I came up to them I asked the coachman where he was going, and he answered that his master was going from Kazan to the Crimea. While I was talking with the coachman his master pulled open the carriage curtains from inside, looked out and saw me. Then he said, " I shall stay the night here, too, but I have not gone into the hut, Tartar houses are so uncomfortable. I have decided to spend the night in the carriage." Then he got out, and as it was a fine evening, we strolled about for a while and talked. He asked me a lot of questions and

talked about himself also, and this is what he told me.
" Until I was sixty-five I was a captain in the navy, but
as I grew old I became the victim of gout—an incurable
disease. So I retired from the service and lived, almost
constantly ill, on a farm of my wife's in the Crimea.
She was an impulsive woman of a volatile disposition, and
a great card-player. She found it boring living with a
sick man, and left me, going off to our daughter in
Kazan, who happened to be married to a civil servant
there. My wife laid hands on all she could, and even
took the servants with her, leaving me with nobody but
an eight-year-old boy, my godson. So I lived alone for
about three years. The boy who served me was a sharp
little fellow, and capable of doing all the household work.
He did my room, heated the stove, cooked the gruel and
got the samovar ready.[15] But at the same time he was
extraordinarily mischievous and full of spirits. He was
incessantly rushing about and banging and shouting
and playing, and up to all sorts of tricks, so that he disturbed me exceedingly. And I, being ill and bored, liked
to read spiritual books all the time. I had one splendid
book by Gregory Palamas, on the Prayer of Jesus. I read
it almost continuously, and I used to say the Prayer to
some extent. But the boy hindered me, and no threats
and no punishment restrained him from indulging in his
pranks. At last I hit upon the following method. I
made him sit on a bench in my room with me, and bade
him say the Prayer of Jesus without stopping. At first
this was extraordinarily distasteful to him, and he tried
all sorts of ways to avoid it, and often fell silent. In

order to make him do my bidding, I kept a cane beside me. When he said the Prayer I quietly read my book, or listened to how he was saying it. But let him stop for a moment, and I showed him the cane, then he got frightened and took to the Prayer again. I found this very peaceful, and quiet reigned in the house. After a while I noticed that now there was no need of the cane; the boy began to do my bidding quite willingly and eagerly. Further, I observed a complete change in his mischievous character: he became quiet and taciturn and performed his household tasks better than before. I was glad of this, and began to allow him more freedom. And what was the result? Well, in the end he got so accustomed to the Prayer that he was saying it almost the whole time, whatever he was doing, and without any compulsion from me at all. When I asked him about it, he answered that he felt an insuperable desire to be saying the Prayer always.

" ' And what are your feelings while doing so?' I asked him.

" ' Nothing,' said he, ' only I feel that it's nice to be saying it.'

" ' How do you mean—nice? "

" ' I don't know how to put it exactly.'

" ' Makes you feel cheerful, do you mean? "

" ' Yes, cheerful.'

" He was twelve years old when the Crimean War broke out, and I went to stay with my daughter at Kazan, taking him with me. Here he lived in the kitchen with the other servants, and this bored him very much.

He would come to me with complaints that the others, playing and joking among themselves, bothered him also, and laughed at him and so prevented him saying his Prayer. In the end, after about three months, he came to me and said, ' I am going home, I'm unbearably sick of this place and all this noise.'

" ' How can you go alone for such a distance and in winter, too ? ' said I. ' Wait, and when I go I'll take you with me.' Next day my boy had vanished.

" We sent everywhere to look for him, but nowhere could he be found. In the end I got a letter from the Crimea, from the people who were on our farm, saying that the boy had been found dead in my empty house on the 4th of April, which was Easter Monday. He was lying peacefully on the floor of my room with his hands folded on his breast, and in that same thin frockcoat that he always went about my house in, and which he was wearing when he went away. And so they buried him in my garden.

" When I heard this news I was absolutely amazed. How had the child reached the farm so quickly ? He started on Feb. 26th, and he was found on April 4th. Even with God's help you want horses to cover 2,000 miles in a month ! Why, it is nearly seventy miles a day ! And in thin clothes, without a passport and without a farthing in his pocket into the bargain ! Even supposing that someone may have given him a lift on the way, still that in itself would be a mark of God's special providence and care for him. That boy of mine, mark you, enjoyed the fruits of prayer," concluded this gentleman, "and here am I, an old man, still not as far on as he."

Later on I said to him, "It is a splendid book, sir, the one by Gregory Palamas, which you said you liked reading. I know it. But it treats rather of the oral Prayer of Jesus. You should read a book called *The Philokalia*. There you will find a full and complete study of how to reach the spiritual Prayer of Jesus in the mind and heart also, and taste the sweet fruit of it." At the same time I showed him my *Philokalia*. I saw that he was pleased to have this advice of mine, and he promised that he would get a copy for himself. And in my own mind I dwelt upon the wonderful ways in which the power of God is shown in this Prayer. What wisdom and teaching there was in the story I had just heard! The cane taught the Prayer to the boy, and what is more, as a means of consolation it became a help to him. Are not our own sorrows and trials which we meet with on the road of prayer in the same way the rod in God's hand? Why then are we so frightened and troubled when our heavenly Father in the fullness of His boundless love lets us see them, and when these rods teach us to be more earnest in learning to pray, and lead us on to consolation which is beyond words?

When I came to the end of the things I had to tell, I said to my spiritual father: "Forgive me, in God's name. I have already chattered far too much. And the holy Fathers call even spiritual talk mere babble if it lasts too long. It is time I went to find my fellow-traveller to Jerusalem. Pray for me, a miserable sinner, that of His great mercy God may bless my journey."

"With all my heart I wish it, dear brother in the Lord," he replied. "May all the all-loving Grace of God shed its light on your path, and go with you, as the Angel Raphael went with Tobias!"

NOTES

[1] *Starets*, pl. *startsi*. A monk distinguished by his great piety, long experience of the spiritual life, and gift for guiding other souls. Lay folk frequently resort to *startsi* for spiritual counsel; and in a monastery a new member of the community is attached to a *starets*, who trains and teaches him.

[2] *Philokalia* (in Russian: *Dobrotolyubie*). "The Love of Spiritual Beauty." The title of the great collection of mystical and ascetic writings by Fathers of the Eastern Orthodox Church, over a period of eleven centuries.

[3] *Dyachok*. A minister whose chief liturgical function is to chant psalms and the Epistle in the Russian Church.

[4] *Mir*. The Assembly of all the peasant householders in a village. It was a very ancient institution, in which the peasants only had a voice, even the great landowners being excluded. The *mir* enjoyed a certain measure of self-government, and elected representatives to the larger peasant assembly of the *volost*, which included several *mirs*. The *starosta* was the elected headman of the *mir*.

[5] *Zavalina*. A bank of earth against the front wall of the house, flat-topped and used as a seat.

[6] *Priests*. The word is *ksendz*, which means a Polish priest of the Roman Catholic Church. The steward, being a Pole, was a Roman Catholic.

[7] *Skhimnik* (fem. *skhimnitsa*). A monk (nun) of the highest grade. The distinction between simple and solemn vows which has arisen in the West, has never found a place in Orthodox Monasticism. In the latter, Religious are of three grades, distinguished by their habit, and the highest grade is pledged to a stricter degree of asceticism and a greater amount of time spent in prayer. The Russian *skhimnik* is the Greek *megaloschemos*.

[8] *Icon*. The icon or sacred picture occupies a prominent position in Orthodox life. In Russia icons are found not only in churches but in public buildings of all sorts, as well as in private houses. In the devout Russian's room the icon will hang or rest on a shelf diagonally across a corner opposite the door, and a reverence will be made to it by a person entering or leaving the room.

[9] *Onoochi*. Long strips of material, generally coarse linen, which

Notes

the Russian peasant wraps round his feet and legs instead of wearing stockings.

¹⁰ *Bashmaki.* A kind of shoes.

¹¹ *Altar.* In Orthodox churches, *altar* is the name of that part of the building which is known in the West as the Sanctuary. What Westerners call the *altar* is in the East the *throne* or *holy table.* In Orthodox phraseology the *throne* stands in the *altar.*

¹² *Batyushka.* " Little Father," a familiar and affectionate form of address, applied usually to priests.

¹³ *Dark water.* The popular name for glaucoma.

¹⁴ The Tartars, of course, being Moslems.

¹⁵ *Samovar.* A sort of urn heated with charcoal to supply hot water for tea.

BIOGRAPHICAL NOTES

ANTHONY THE GREAT was born about A.D. 250 in Egypt. As a young man he adopted the solitary life of the ascetic and was perhaps the first to withdraw into the desert to live a hermit life. His influence spread widely and he kept in touch with his friend St. Athanasius the Great who wrote his *Life*.

BASIL THE GREAT. Bishop of Cæsarea in Cappadocia in the fourth century. A great writer and preacher, he was a reformer also in the spheres of the Liturgy and the monastic life. The " Liturgy of St. Basil " is used by the Orthodox on Sundays in Lent and a few other days. Orthodox monks and nuns follow the Rule of St. Basil.

BLESSED DIADOKH was Bishop of Photice in Epirus. Victor, Bishop of Utica, writing in the preface to his *History of the Barbarity of the Vandals* about the year 490, calls himself the pupil of Diadokh, and speaks in high praise of his spiritual writings. Diadokh, therefore, flourished in the second half of the fifth century. His signature appears among those attached to the letter from the Epirote bishops to the Emperor Leo. But nothing more is known of him.

CALLISTUS THE PATRIARCH, a disciple of Gregory the Sinaite in the *skeet* of Magoola on Mount Athos, led the ascetic life for twenty-eight years in company with one Mark, and especially with Ignatius, with whom he had so great a friendship that " it appeared as though but one spirit was in the two of them." Later, after he had been made Patriarch, he was passing by Mount Athos on his way to Serbia, and during his stay in the Holy Mountain one Maxium foretold his early death. " This *starets* will not see his flock again, for behind him can be heard the funeral hymn, ' Blessed are they that are undefiled in the way.' " On his arrival in Serbia Callistus did, in fact, die. Gregory Palamas, in his treatise on the Jesus Prayer, speaks very highly of the writings of Callistus and Ignatius on the same subject. They lived in the middle of the 14th century.

CHRYSOSTOM. The most famous of the Greek Fathers. He was born about A.D. 345 at Antioch in Syria, and was trained as a lawyer. At the age of thirty-five, however, he was baptized and later ordained. He became Archbishop of Constantinople, in which office he led a life of ascetic simplicity, and was celebrated for his writings and sermons. (The name means " golden-mouthed.") He died in 407.

EPHRAEM THE SYRIAN. The great Syriac writer, poet, and commentator, of the 4th century. He was ordained deacon but in humility refused any higher order. The bulk of his vast output of literary work was written in verse and upon many varieties of theological subjects. He was a notable champion of orthodoxy especially against Marcion and in defence of the creed of Nicaea. He died at Edessa about A.D. 373.

GREGORY PALAMAS. A 14th-century monk of Athos and the outstanding defender on dogmatic grounds of Hesychasm (see SIMEON THE NEW THEOLOGIAN), to which the Council of St. Sophia gave the official approval of the Orthodox Church in 1351. Palamas died as Archbishop of Thessalonika in 1359.

GREGORY THE SINAITE took the habit in the monastery on Mount Sinai about the year 1330. Later he went to Mount Athos, where he stimulated the contemplative life. He also founded three great Lavras in Macedonia, and taught the practice of unceasing prayer. Callistus, the Patriarch of Constantinople, a former pupil of his, wrote his *Life*.

INNOCENT was one of the great Russian missionaries of the 18th century. By the appointment of Peter the Great he was consecrated to be the first Bishop of Pekin, but the Chinese refused to allow the establishment of the bishopric in that city, and Innocent became Bishop of Irkutsk. He laboured as a missionary bishop for some ten years and died at Irkutsk in 1731.

ISIKHI was a native of Jerusalem and in his early years a pupil of Gregory the Theologian. He retired to one of the hermitages in Palestine for some years, but became a priest in the year 412 and established a great reputation as a teacher and interpreter of Holy Scripture. The date of his death is given as 432–433.

JOHN OF DAMASCUS. The famous theologian and hymn-writer who lived in Palestine in the 8th century and is honoured in East and West alike. His great work, *The Fountain of Knowledge*, is concerned with religious philosophy and dogmatic theology. A man of immense learning in many fields, he is well known for his three treatises in defence of the " Images " (Icons). One or two of St. John Damascene's very large output of " hymns " are to be found in English hymn-books, *e.g.*, " Come ye faithful, raise the strain," " The Day of Resurrection," " What sweet of life endureth."

JOHN KARPATHISKY. Nothing certain seems to be known about this writer. But Photius speaks of reading a book which contained, beside writings of Diadokh and Nil, a section by John Karpathisky entitled, " A consoling word to the monks who have turned to him for consolation from India." This has been taken to imply that he was a contemporary of Diadokh and Nil, and belongs to the fifth century. Karpathos is an island between Rhodes and Crete, and he was presumably either a native of the island or lived there for some time.

KASSIAN THE ROMAN was born between 350 and 360, probably in the neighbourhood of Marseilles. His parents were well-known people and wealthy, and he received a good education. He went to the East and became a monk at Bethlehem. About two years later, hearing of the ascetic achievements of the Egyptian Fathers, he went with a friend, German, to visit them. This was about the year 390. Except for a short visit to their own monastery in 397, the friends stayed among the Egyptian hermits until the year 400. In that year they went to Constantinople, where they were received by St. John Chrysostom, who ordained Kassian deacon and German priest. The two friends were among those who were sent in 405 to Rome by the friends of Chrysostom to seek help for him when he was imprisoned. Kassian did not return to the East, but spent the rest of his life in his native land, still practising the severe asceticism he had learned in Egypt. He left some twelve volumes on the constitution and ordering of the monastic life, written, it is said, at the request of many in whom the monasteries he founded inspired great admiration. He died in 435 and is commemorated by the Orthodox on February 29.

MACARIUS THE GREAT (of Egypt) was the son of a peasant and himself a shepherd. Feeling a strong attraction to the hermit life, he retired to a cell near his own village and later withdrew with some other monks into the desert on the borders of Libya and Egypt. He was ordained priest and became the head of the brotherhood. He suffered at the hands of the Arians for his rigid orthodoxy, and died in the year 390 in the desert at the age of ninety, having spent sixty years in solitude. Miraculous power and the gift of prophecy were attributed to him. He left numerous writings on the spiritual life. His relics are venerated at Amalfi.

Biographical Notes

MARK THE PODVIZHNIK was one of the most notable of the Egyptian Fathers, but little is known of his life. He is said to have been mild and gentle, to have had such love of the study of Holy Scriptures that he knew both the Old and New Testaments by heart. He is supposed to have lived beyond the age of a hundred years, and to have died at the beginning of the fifth century. He left behind him the memory of his deep spirituality and of his devotion to Holy Communion; but few of the numerous writings ascribed to him have survived.

NICEPHORUS THE RECLUSE was a great ascetic of Mount Athos, who died shortly before 1340. He was the director of Gregory of Salonika (Palamas).

NICETAS STETHATUS was a presbyter of the Studium in the eleventh century, and pupil of St. Simeon the New Theologian, whose virtues and wisdom he absorbed to such an extent that he was said to shine as the twin sun of his teacher.

PHILOTHEUS was *igumen* (abbot) of the Slav monastic community on Mount Sinai, but at what date is not known.

SIMEON THE NEW THEOLOGIAN died in the first half of the eleventh century. He was a monk of the Studium in Constantinople, and a great visionary and mystic. His visions began when he was a boy of fourteen. *The Method* (*i.e.*, the *Hesychast* method of prayer, the way of using the Jesus Prayer) has been attributed to him, but Hausherr gives reasons for concluding that he was not the author, though his influence contributed to the spread of the method. Various explanations of his name have been given, and it has sometimes been translated as " Simeon the Young, the theologian "; but according to Nicetas Stethatus, who wrote his life, the name recalls St. John the Divine, and so would mean " the new St. John." An examination of the whole subject of the *Hesychast* method and its connection with Simeon is to be found in *Orientalia Christiana*, vol. ix, No. 36, June–July, 1927.

ST. JOHN OF THE LADDER, or KLIMAX, lived for forty years in a cave at the foot of Mount Sinai. Then he became Abbot of the Monastery on the Mountain. He died about 600. He wrote a book called *The Ladder to Paradise*, and from this he derives his name. *The Ladder* has been translated into English.

THEOLEPT. A monk of Mount Athos, and later Metropolitan of Philadelphia. Among his pupils at Athos was Gregory Palamas.

SOLOVETSKY ISLE

ARKHANGEL

KAZAN

MOSCOW

SMOLENSK
VILNA
SHKLOV
MOGILEV

OREL

BYELGEROD

KIEV
ZHITOMIR
POCHAEV
BYELAYA
TSERKOV

KAMENETS PODOLSK

ODESSA

ASTRAKHAN

ENGLISH   0   100   200   300   400   500   MILES

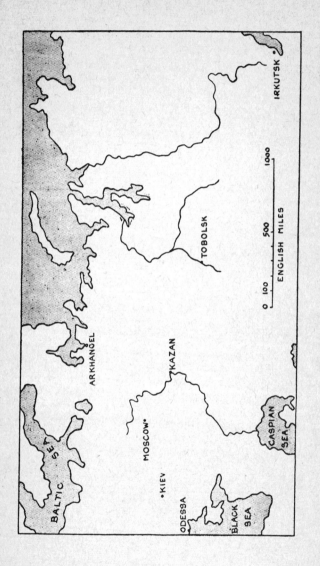